Olympiad ACE

A Comprehensive Practice Book

for School Olympiads & Talent Search Exams

REASONING

Class 1

BLOOM

Olympiad ACE

A Comprehensive Practice Book

for School Olympiads & Talent Search Exams

REASONING

Class 1

by

Ruchika

Olympiad ACE

BLOOM
Bloom Cap Edu Ventures Pvt. Ltd.

Administrative & Production Office

'Ramchhaya' 4577/15, Agarwal Road, Darya Ganj, New Delhi -110002
Tele: 011- 47630600, 43518550

PRICE: ₹125.00

Published by Arihant Publications (I) Ltd.

For further information about the books log on to
www.bloomcap.org

Follow us on

Preface

"Future belongs to those Who prepares for it today"

School Olympiads are National & International level competitions conducted by different Government, Non-Government & Educational Organisations with the purpose of making the children ready to face competitive exams.

The challenging Questions asked in Olympiads motivate them to learn more & more and bring out the best result with improved academic performance. The Awards & Scholarship offered by Olympiads motivate children to aspire & strive for doing better and emerge out to be the best.

Science Olympiads

Being a Scientist or Engineer or Doctor has always been a dream of each school going child. A good command over Science is a must for any of these. Questions of Science Olympiads are structured to help students to develop scientific temperament & motivate them to understand the concepts of science. They also focuses on improving existing knowledge of a student by adding more information.

'Bloom Science Olympiad Study Book Class 1' is a perfect resource to Study & Practice for Olympiad Exams and other National & State Level Talent Search Exams & Other Competitions.

Some Special Features of Bloom Science Olympiad Study Books are;

- Chapterwise Exercises having different types of Objective Questions; Analytical, Applications, Remembering etc, at par with the Olympiad Level.
- Detailed Explanation for each question.
- Olympiad Pattern Practice Sets at the end.

This book is prepared by Expert Panel with the utmost care, still if you have any suggestions regarding its improvement then feel free to contact us at support@bloomcap.org. We will try to inculcate your suggestions in the further editions.

Contents

Chapter 01

Matching Pairs

To understand the concept of 'Matching Pairs', Let see some examples.

Directions (Ex. Nos. 1-4) There are certain relationship between the pair of alphabets/words/figures/numbers given on either side of (::). Identify the relationship of given pair and find the matching term.

EXAMPLE 1

(a)  (b)  (c)  (d) 

Sol. *(b)* As 'A' for Apple, similarly 'H' for Hen. Hence, option (b) is correct.

EXAMPLE 2

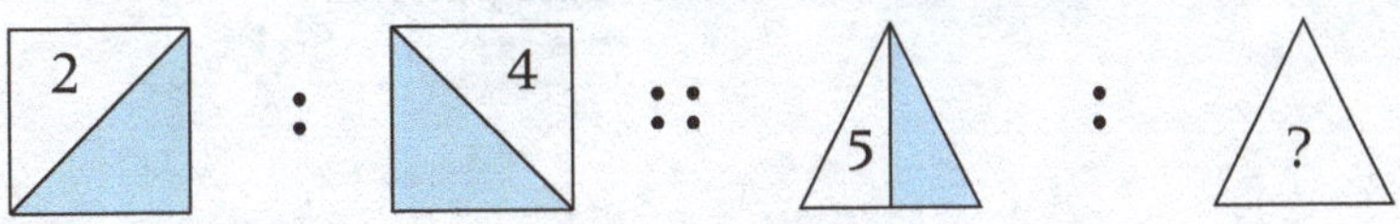

(a) 8 (b) 15

(c) 10 (d) 12

Sol. *(c)* As, $2 \times 2 = 4$ Similarly, $5 \times 2 = 10$

Hence, option (c) is correct.

EXAMPLE 3  :  ::  : ?

(a)  (b)  (c)  (d) 

Sol. *(c)* As cat and cow are animals. Similarly, crow and parrot are birds.

Hence, option (c) is correct.

From the above example we conclude that the "Matching pairs' means similarity or equality between the pairs'.

EXAMPLE 4 (F S I H) :  :: (B A E R) : ?

(a)  (b)  (c)  (d) 

Sol. *(b)* Combination of letters in first figure is the name of the animal in the second figure.

Hence, option (b) is correct.

The following steps can help to solve matching pair questions.

Step 1. Look the first pair.

Step 2. Find similarity between them.

Step 3. Apply the similarity on question pair.

Step 4. Choose the answer which follow the same pattern.

Let's Practice

Directions (Q. Nos. 1-7) There is a certain relationship between the pair of letters/ words/figures given on either side of (::). Identify the relationship of given pair and find the matching term.

1. SAT : 3 : CLAT : ?

   (a) 5 (b) 6
   (c) 4 (d) 7

2. MON : NOO :: SON : ?

   (a) UOO (b) TOO
   (c) MOO (d) ROO

3. P : Q :: I : ?

   (a) K (b) J
   (c) L (d) H

4. 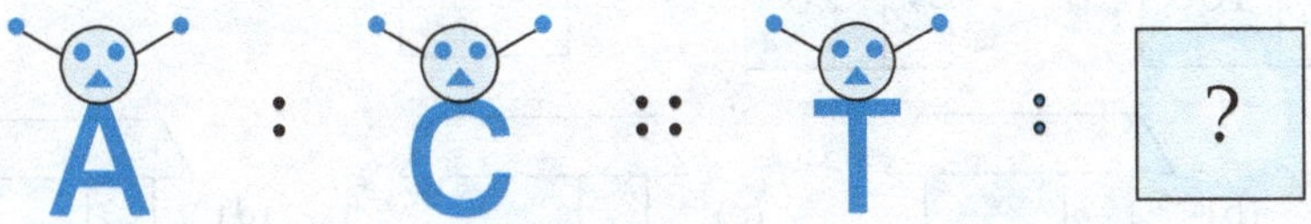

   (a)  (b) 
   (c)  (d) 

5. AB : YZ :: CD : ?

   (a) UW (b) XW
   (c) XY (d) WX

6. 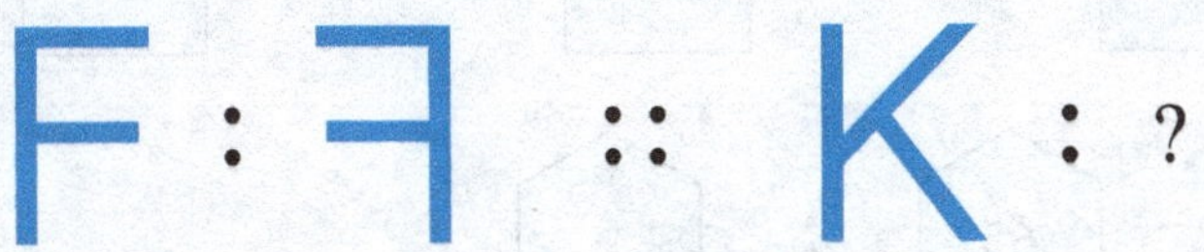

   (a) L (b) E
   (c)  (d) M

7. 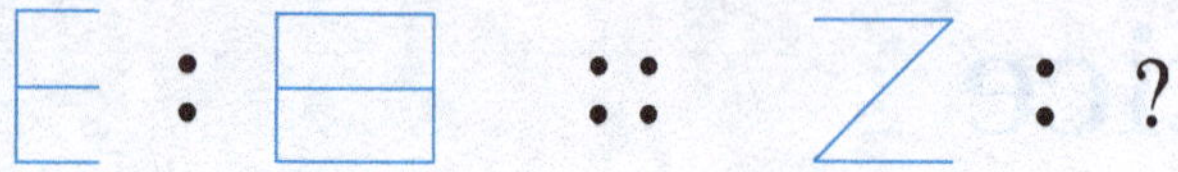

(a) 
(b) 
(c) 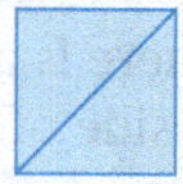
(d) 

Directions (Q. Nos. 8-14) There are certain relationship between the pair of numbers/figures given on either side of (::). Identify the relationship of given pair and find the matching term.

8. 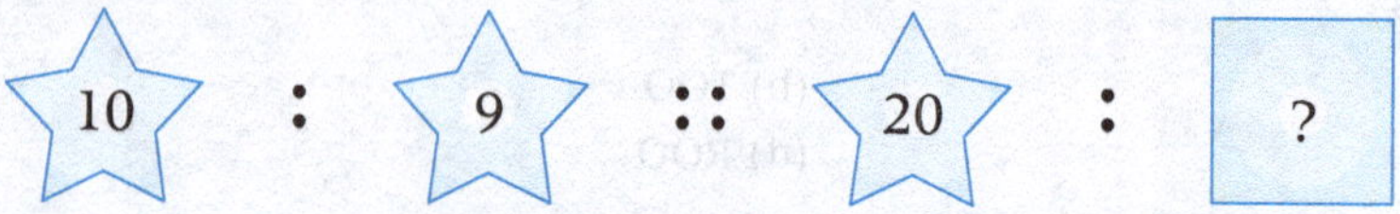

(a) 

(b) 

(c) 

(d) 

9. 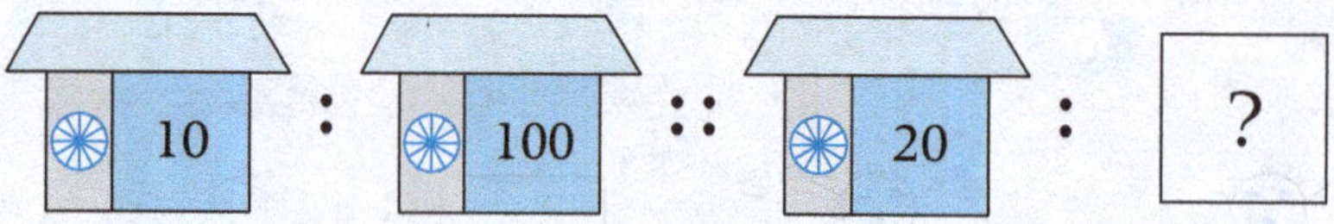

(a) 

(b) 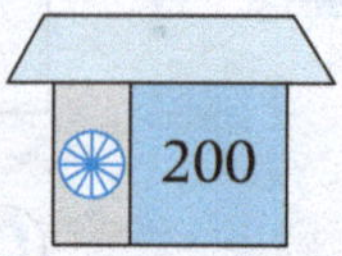

(c) 

(d) 

10. 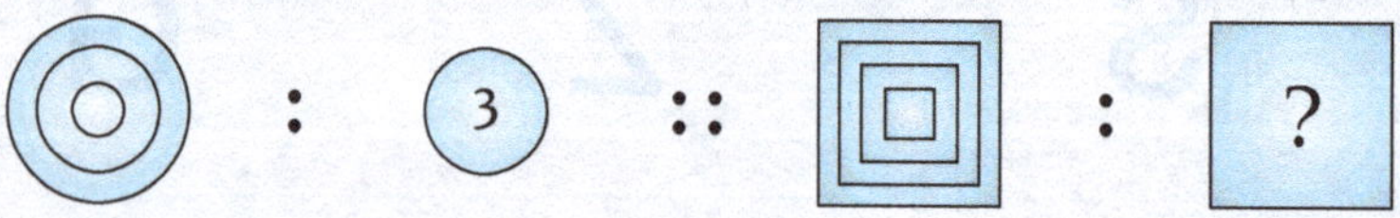

(a) 

(b) 

(c) 

(d) 

11. 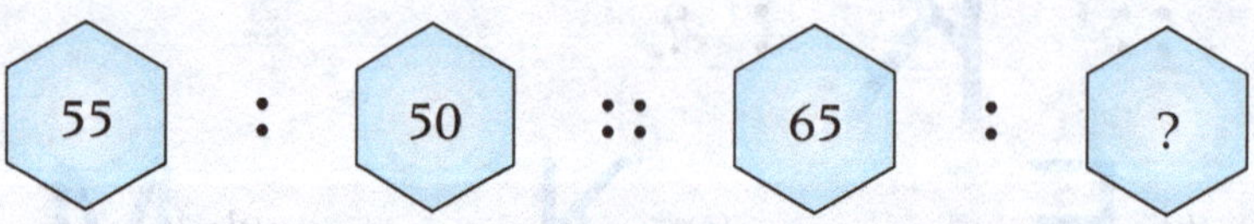

(a) 

(b) 

(c) 

(d) 

12.  : 7 ::  : ?

(a) 9 (b) 10 (c) 8 (d) 6

13. 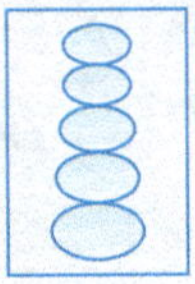 : 5 ::  : ?

(a) 3 (b) 7 (c) 9 (d) 10

14. Twenty : 40 :: Thirty : ?

(a) 10 (b) 60 (c) 6 (d) 26

Directions (Q. Nos. 15-30) There is a certain relationship between the pair of figures given on either side of (::). Identify the relationship of given pair and find the matching term.

15.  :  ::  : ?

(a)  (b)  (c)  (d) 

16. 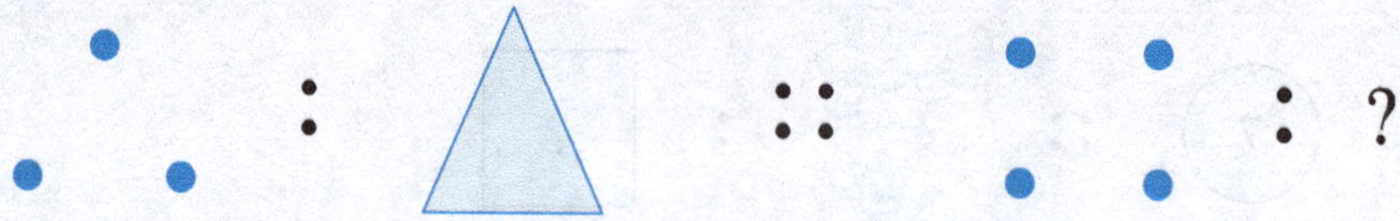

17. 

18. 

19. 

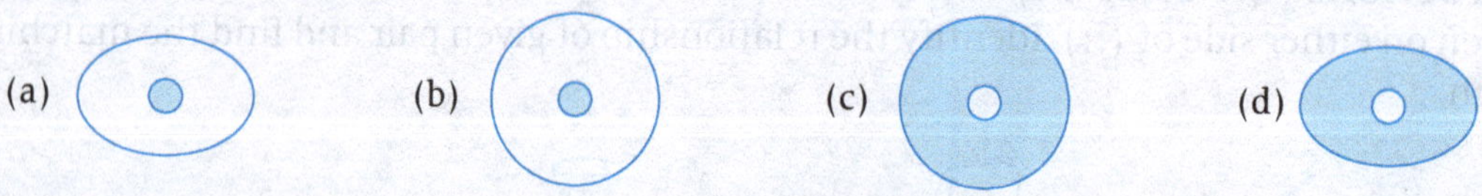

20. 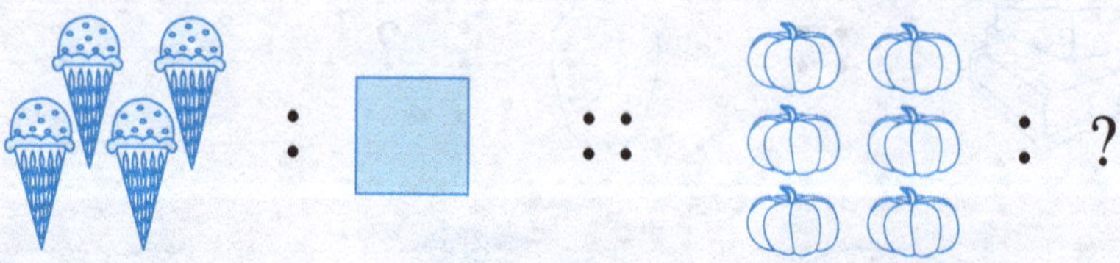

21. 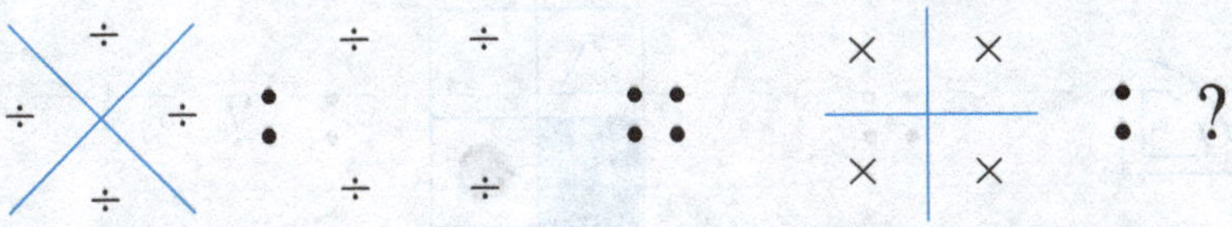

(a)  (b)  (c)  (d) 

22. 

(a) 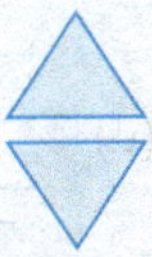 (b) 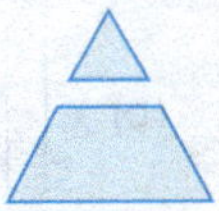 (c)  (d) 

23. 

(a)  (b)  (c)  (d) 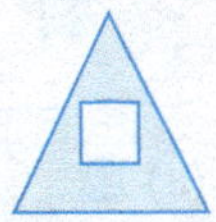

24. 

(a)  (b)  (c)  (d) 

25. 

(a)  (b)  (c) 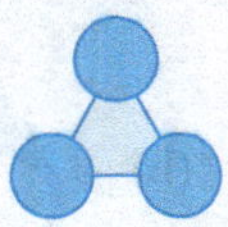 (d) 

26. 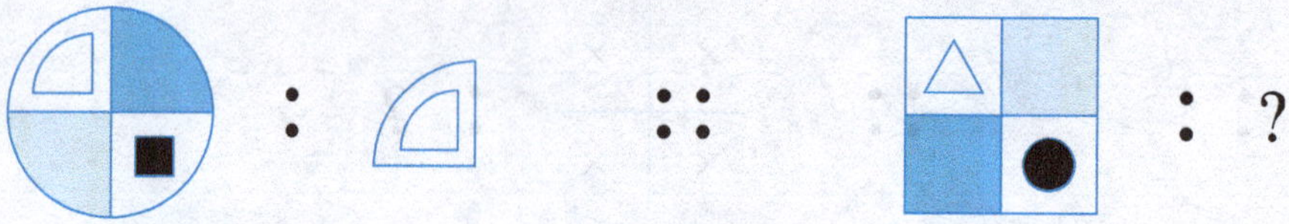

(a)  (b)  (c) 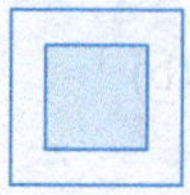 (d) 

27. 

(a)  (b)  (c)  (d) 

28. 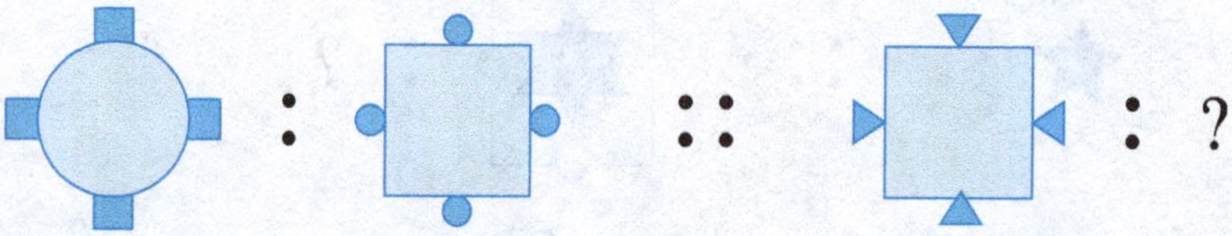

(a)  (b) 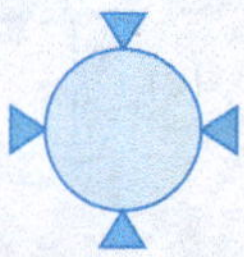 (c)  (d) 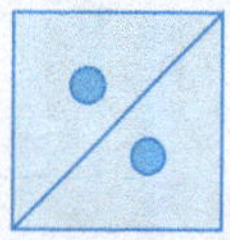

29.  : Circle ::  : ?

(a) Cube (b) Sphere (c) Cylinder (d) Cone

30.  : 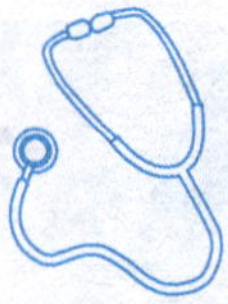 ::  : ?

(a)  (b)  (c)  (d) 

Chapter 02

Odd One Out

To understand the concept of "odd one out" let us see some examples.

Directions (Ex. Nos. 1-4) In the following question a set of alphabets/figures is given. Among these all have some common things except one. Choose the option which differs from all the others in the given set.

EXAMPLE 1 (a) YZ (b) ST (c) IK (d) MN

Sol. *(c)* Except option (c), all are immediate letters of English alphabet.

EXAMPLE 2 (a) 

(b) 

(c) 

(d) 

Sol. *(c)* Except option (c) all the given numbers present in pair. Hence, option (c) is correct.

Directions (Ex.Nos. 3 and 4) In the following questions a set of figures is given. Among these all have some common things except one. Students are required to choose the option which differs from all others in the given set.

EXAMPLE 3 (a)  (b)  (c)  (d) 

Sol. *(a)* Except option (a), all are used to contain water or liquid. Thus, option (a) is different from others. Hence, option (a) is correct.

EXAMPLE 4 (a)  (b)  (c)  (d) 

Sol. *(c)* Except option (c), all design show smily face and in option (c) the face is sad. Hence, option (c) is correct.

From the above examples we conclude that the "Odd one out" is to find the different from other in particular manner/group.

Students are suggested to follow these steps to find answer quickly.

Step 1 : Look carefully each and every picture.
Step 2 : Find the common things like shapes, size, etc.
Step 3 : Select the figure which is not related to other.
Step 4 : Odd figure is your answer.

Let's Practice

Directions (Q. Nos. 1-7) Find the odd one out from the given letters/words figures and numbers.

1. (a) GGg (b) PPp (c) KKk (d) MmM

2. (a) 

(b) 

(c) 

(d) 

3. (a) 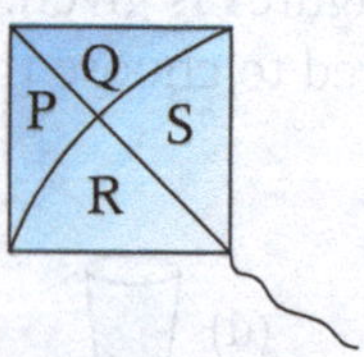

(b) 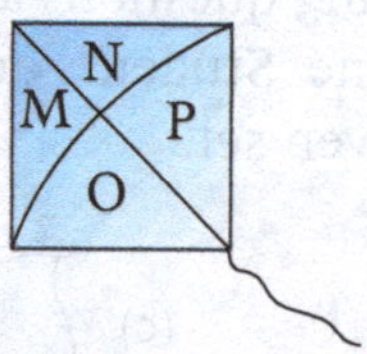

(c) 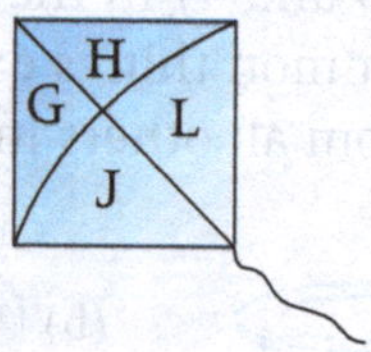

(d) 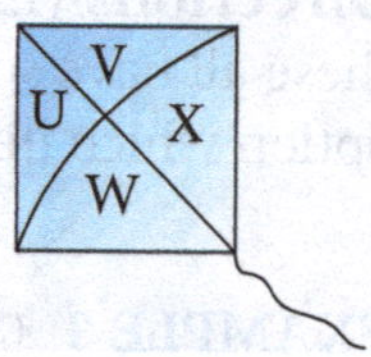

4. (a) Orange (b) Pink (c) Green (d) Grass

5. (a) A (b) E (c) I (d) M

6. (a) January (b) March (c) May (d) April

7. (a) Apple (b) Banana (c) Guava (d) Potato

Directions (Q. Nos. 8-11) Find the odd one out from the given numbers/figures.

8. (a) 

(b) 

(c) 

(d) 

9. (a) 

(b) 

(c) 

(d) 

10. (a) 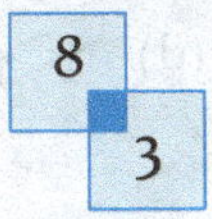

(b) 

(c) 

(d) 

11. (a) 

(b) 

(c) 

(d) 

12. (a) 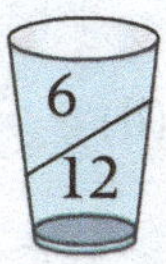

(b) 

(c) 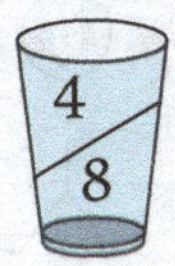

(d) 

Directions (Q.Nos. 13-25) *Find the odd one out from the given figures.*

13. (a)  (b)  (c)  (d) 

14. (a)  (b)  (c)  (d) 

15. (a)  (b)  (c)  (d) 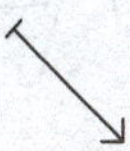

16. (a) 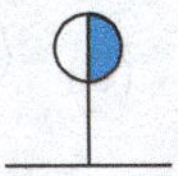 (b) 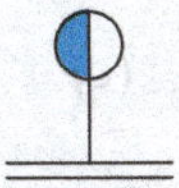 (c) 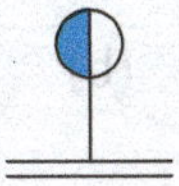 (d) 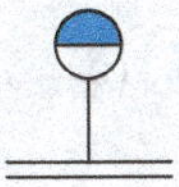

17. (a)  (b) 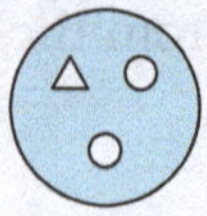 (c)  (d) 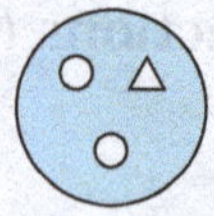

18. (a)  (b)  (c)  (d) 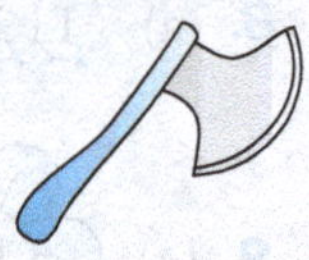

19. (a)  (b) 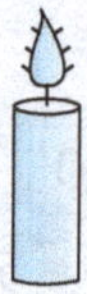 (c)  (d) 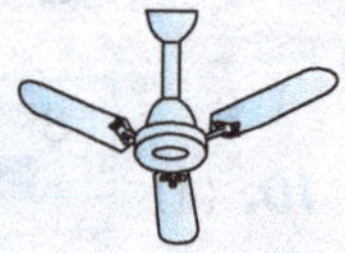

20. (a)  (b) 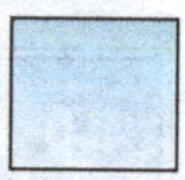 (c)  (d) 

21. (a)  (b)  (c)  (d) 

22. (a) 

(b) 

(c) 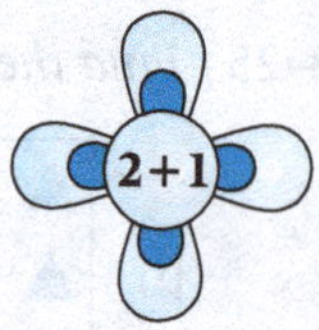

(d) 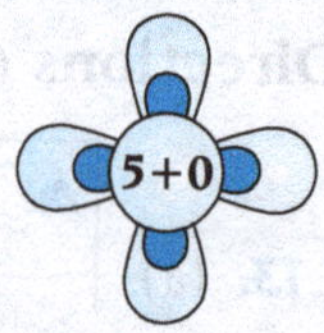

23. (a) 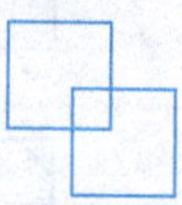 (b)  (c) 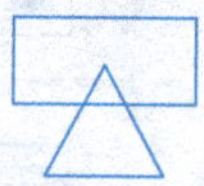 (d) 

24. (a) 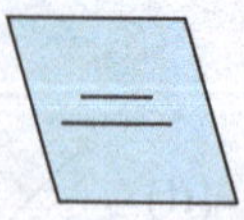 (b) 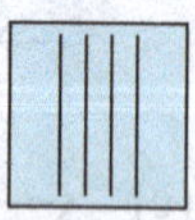 (c)  (d) 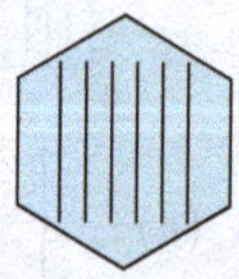

25. (a) 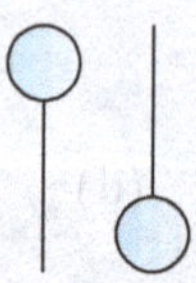 (b) 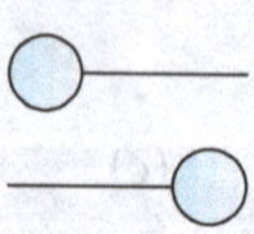 (c) 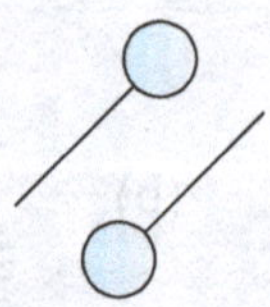 (d) 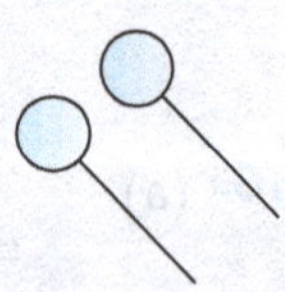

Chapter 03

What Comes Next?

To understand the concept of "What Comes Next". Let us see some examples.

Directions (Ex. Nos. 1-4) Which letter/word/number/figure comes next from the given options?

EXAMPLE 1

(a) 

(b) 

(c) 

(d) 

Sol. *(c)* Letters in flower are arranged in increasing alphabetical order, but one letter is skipped in between the two flowers. Which is in option (c).
Thus option (c) is correct.

EXAMPLE 2

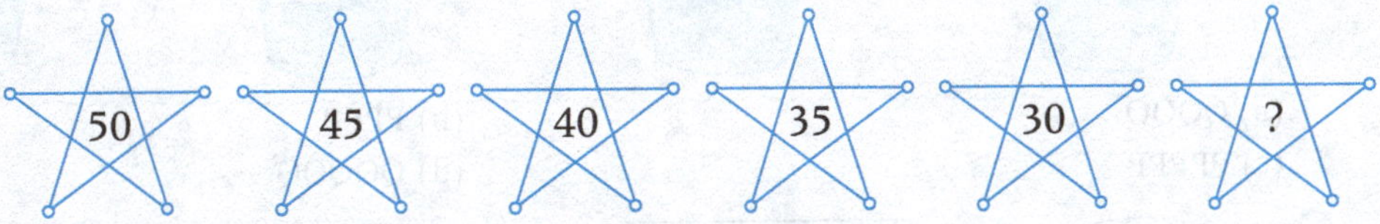

(a) 25 (b) 35 (c) 20 (d) 31

Sol. *(a)* In the given pattern each time number is decreased by 5.

$$50 \xrightarrow{-5} 45 \xrightarrow{-5} 40 \xrightarrow{-5} 35 \xrightarrow{-5} 30 \xrightarrow{-5} \boxed{25}$$

Hence, option (a) is correct.

EXAMPLE 3

(a) ₹ 70 (b) ₹ 80 (c) ₹ 95 (d) ₹ 62

Sol. *(a)* In the given pattern each time the amount of balloon is increase by ₹ 10.

$$30 \xrightarrow{+10} 40 \xrightarrow{+10} 50 \xrightarrow{+10} 60 \xrightarrow{+10} \boxed{70}$$

Hence, option (a) is correct.

EXAMPLE 4

(a)  (b)  (c)  (d) 

Sol. *(b)* The size of caterpillar increases in each step.

Let's Practice

Directions (Q. Nos. 1-7) *Which letter/word/pattern comes next from the given options?*

1. 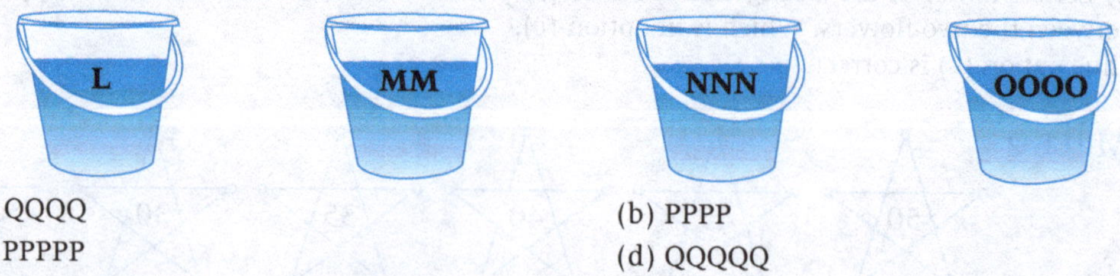

(a) QQQQ (b) PPPP
(c) PPPPP (d) QQQQQ

2. 

(a) Monday (b) Wednesday
(c) Friday (d) Saturday

3. 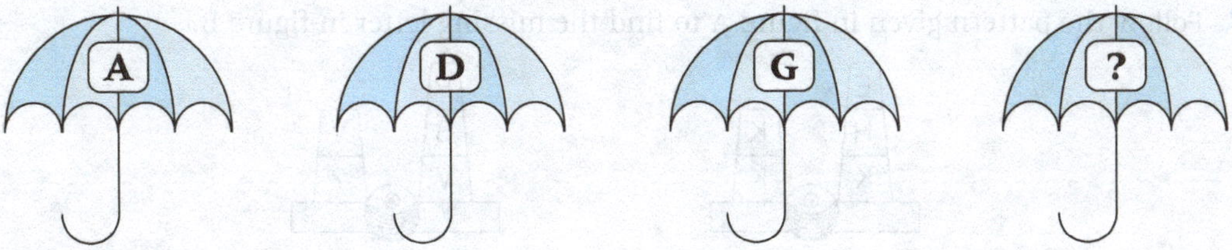

(a) K
(b) J
(c) I
(d) H

4. 

(a) TN
(b) EN
(c) TE
(d) NT

5. 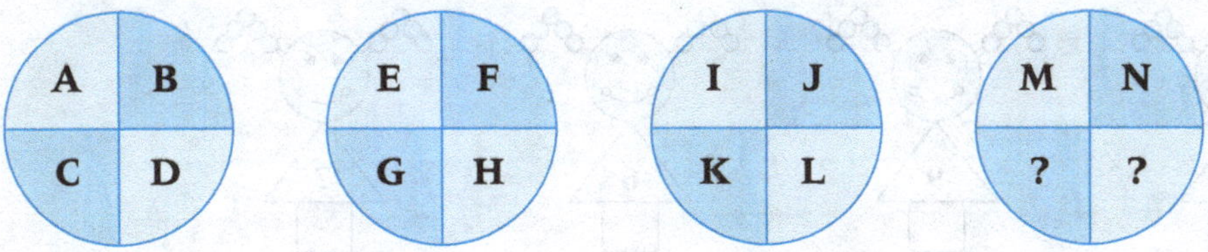

(a) RQ
(b) OP
(c) QR
(d) PO

6. 

(a) T
(b) U
(c) P
(d) V

7. 

(a) JUNE
(b) JULY
(c) DECEMBER
(d) AUGUST

8. Follow the pattern given in figure A to find the missing letter in figure B.

A B

(a) K (b) T (c) U (d) V

Directions (Q. Nos. 9-15) Which number comes next from the given options ?

9. 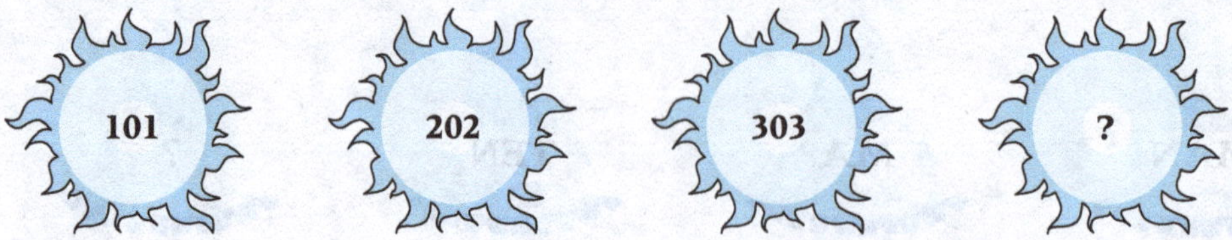

(a) 505 (b) 404
(c) 606 (d) 707

10. 

(a) 8 (b) 7 (c) 3 (d) 1

11. 

(a) 50 (b) 500 (c) 05 (d) 005

12. 

(a) 8 (b) Eight (c) 9 (d) Six

13. 

(a) 15 (b) 1 (c) 18 (d) 12

14. If same rule is followed in A, B and C, then find the missing number.

3	6
12	9

A

2	?
8	6

B

1	2
4	3

C

(a) 3 (b) 4 (c) 5 (d) 10

Directions (Q. Nos. 15-25) Which figure/pattern/shape comes next?

15.  ?

(a) (b)  (c)  (d)

16.  ?

(a)  (b)  (c) 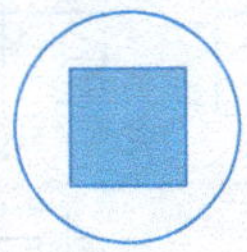 (d) 

17.  ?

(a)  (b)  (c)  (d) 

18. 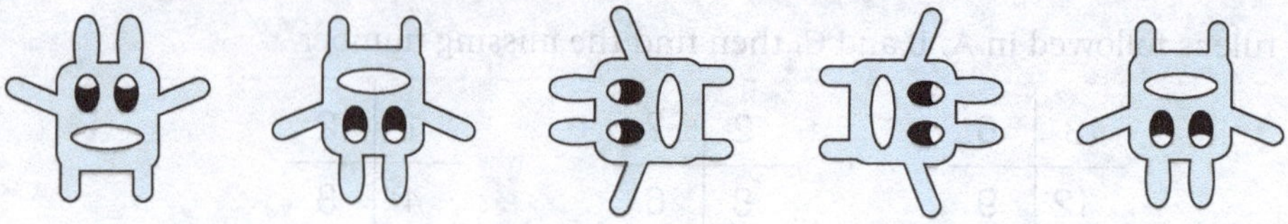 ?

(a)  (b)  (c)  (d) 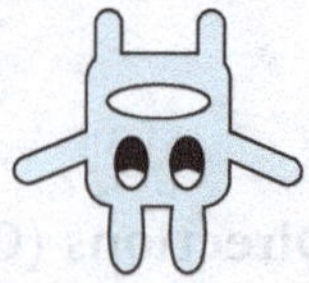

19. 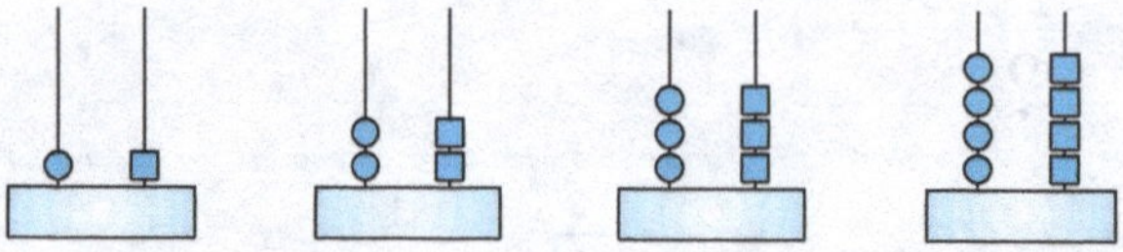 ?

(a) 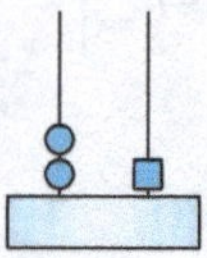 (b) 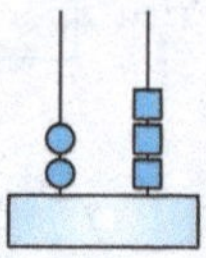 (c) 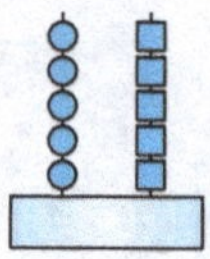 (d) 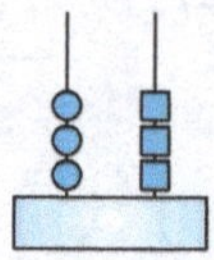

20. 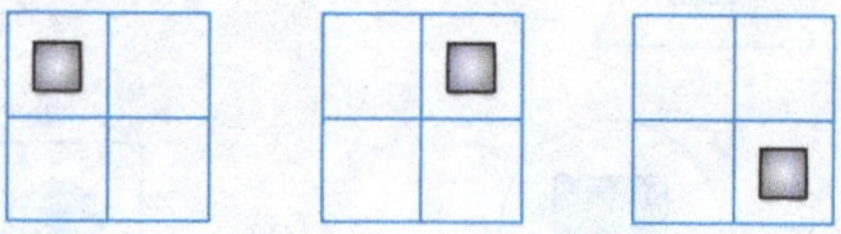 ?

(a) 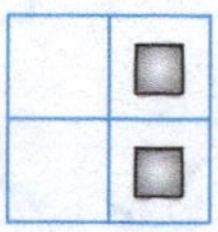 (b) 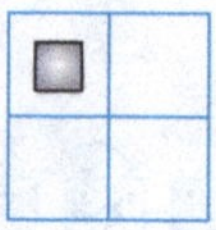 (c) 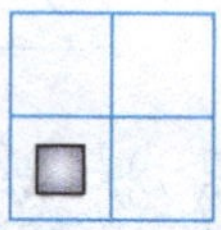 (d) 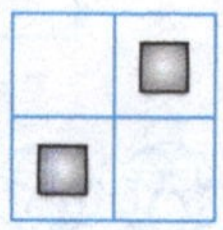

21.  ?

(a)  (b)  (c)  (d) 

22. 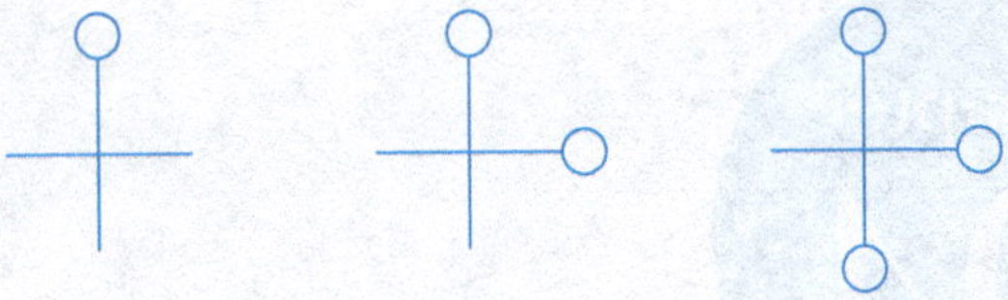 ?

(a) 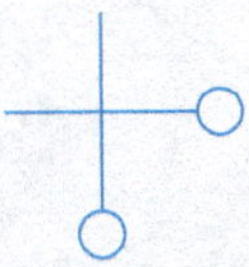 (b) 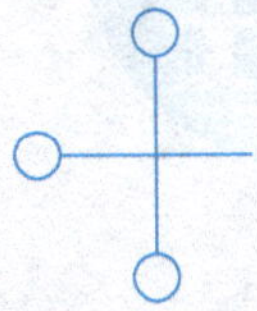 (c) 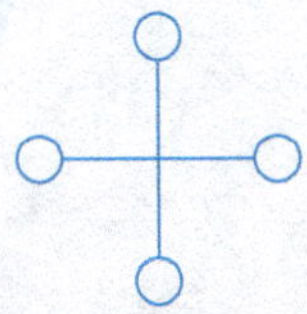 (d) 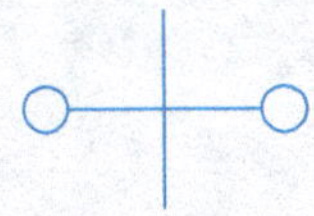

23.  ?

(a)  (b) 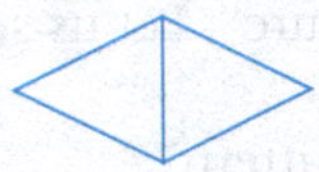 (c) 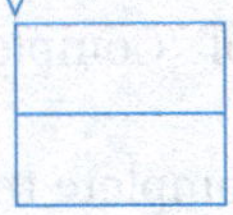 (d) 

24.  ?

(a)  (b)  (c)  (d) 

25. 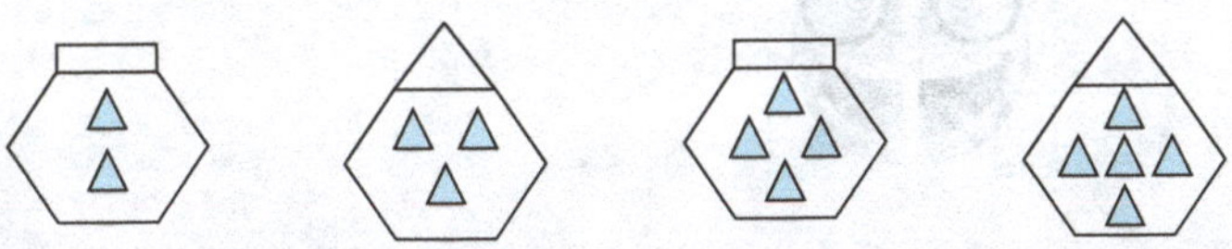 ?

(a) 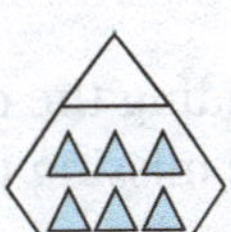 (b) 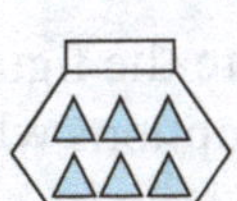 (c) 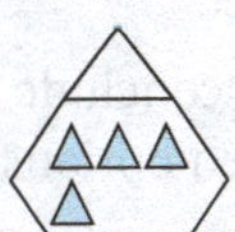 (d) 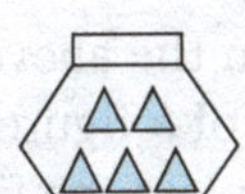

Chapter 04

Complete the Figure

To understand the concept of "Complete the figure". Let us see some examples.

EXAMPLE 1 Which will complete the given pattern?

(a)  (b)  (c)  (d) 

Sol. *(d)* From the given alternatives we see that, the figure in option (d) will complete the given pattern and it will look as shown below.

Hence, option (d) is correct.

From the above example we conclude that "complete the figure" means finding the missing part of a figure from the given options. So that the options when put at the missing place will complete the figure.

The following steps can help to find answer figure easily.

Step 1 : Look at the question figure very carefully.

Step 2 : Eliminate all options which are not look like question figure.

Step 3 : Select the answer figure and compare with missing part of the question figure.

If question figure and option figure will make together a complete picture, then answer option is correct.

EXAMPLE 2 Ronnie draw a picture on him drawing book. Which will complete the given pattern?

(a) 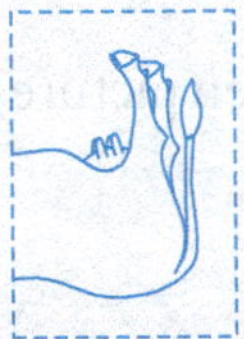 (b)  (c)  (d) 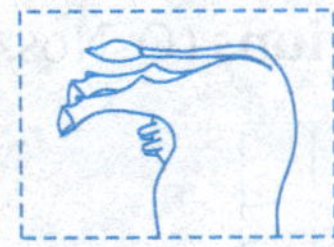

Sol. *(b)* From the given alternatives we see that, the figure in option (b) will complete the given pattern and it will look as shown below.

Hence, option (b) is correct.

EXAMPLE 3 Complete the figure pattern given below.

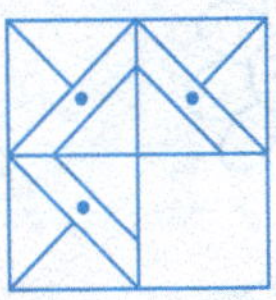

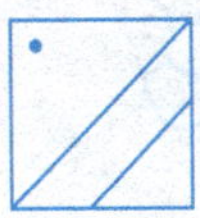
(a)

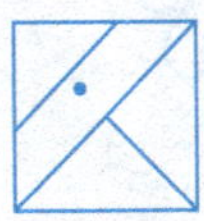
(b)

(c)

(d)

Sol. *(b)* From the given alternatives we see that the figure in option (b) will complete the given pattern and it will look as shown below.

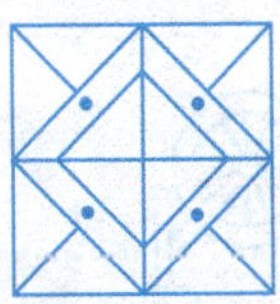

Let's Practice

Directions (Q. Nos. 1-12) Find the other half of the given picture from the options provided.

1.

2.

3.

4.

5.

6.

7.

8.

9.  (a)  (b)  (c)  (d) 

10.  (a)  (b)  (c)  (d) 

Directions (Q. Nos. 11-14) Complete the figure patterns given below.

11.  (a)  (b) 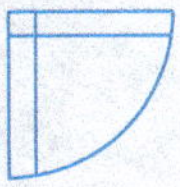 (c)  (d) 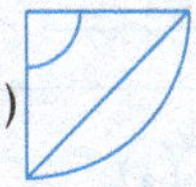

12. 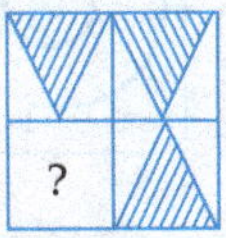
(X)
(a)  (b)  (c)  (d) 

13. 
(X)
(a)  (b)  (c)  (d) 

14. 
(X)
(a)  (b)  (c)  (d) 

Direction (Q. Nos. 15-23) Find the other half of the given letter/word/number picture from the options provided.

15.  (a)  (b)  (c) 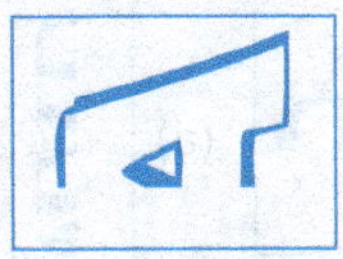 (d) 

16.  (a)  (b)  (c)  (d) 

17.

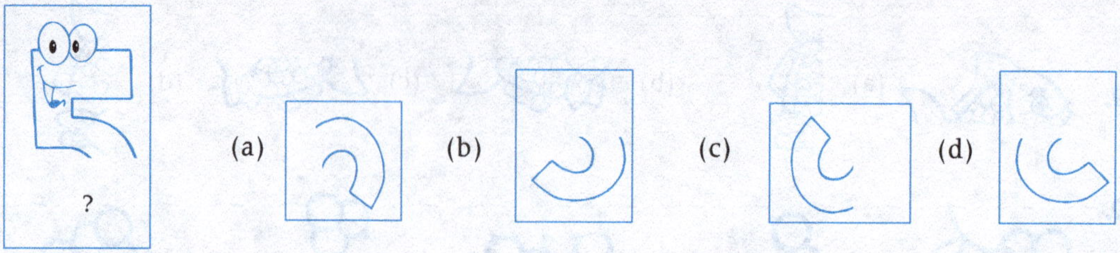

18.

19.

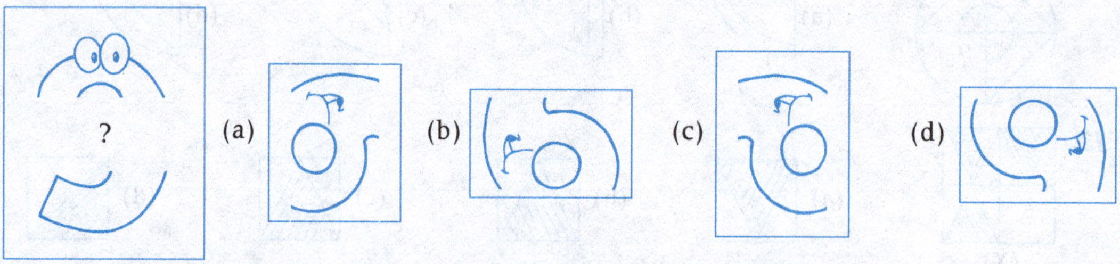

20.

21.

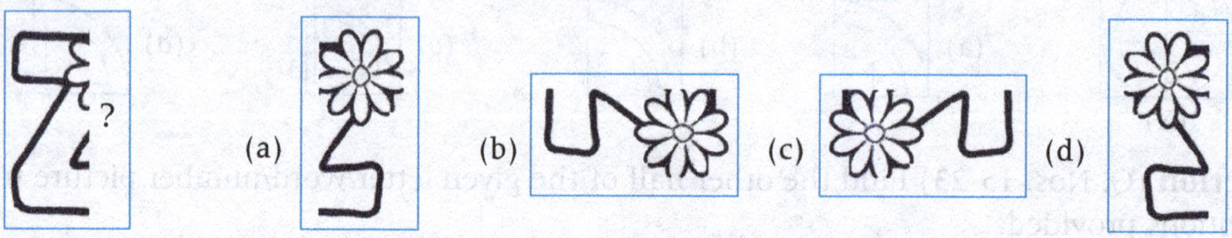

22.

23.

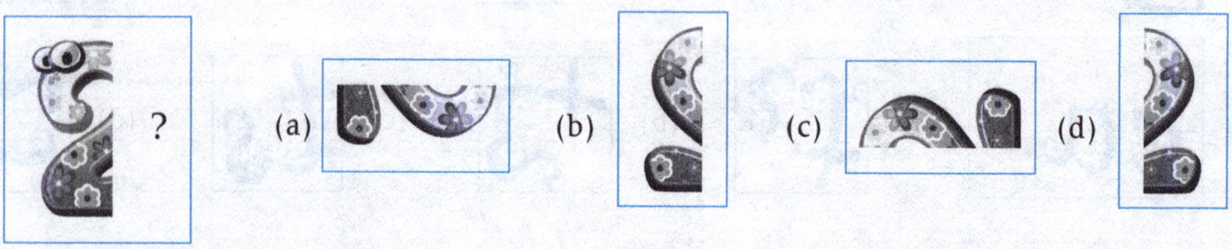

Chapter

05

Find Similar Shapes

To understand the concept of "Find Similar Shapes" Let us discuss some examples.

EXAMPLE 1 Which object is same as the given figure?

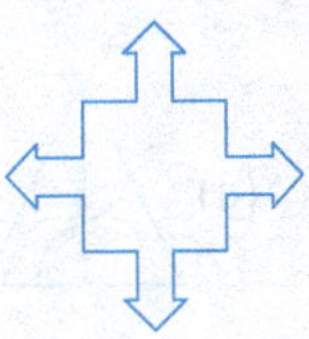 (a) 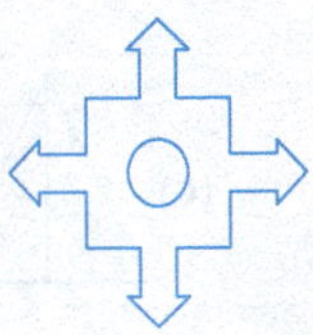 (b) 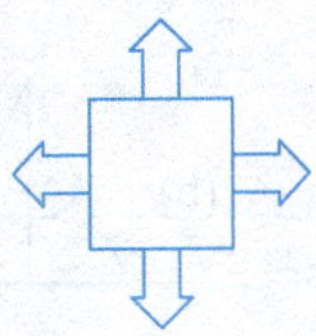 (c) 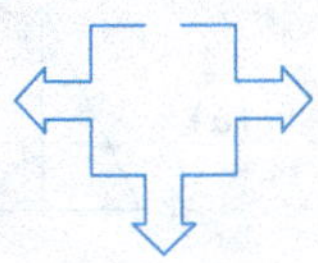 (d) 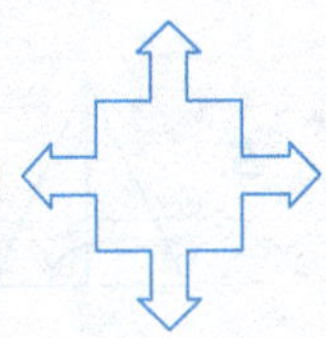

Sol. *(d)* By checking options, it is concluded that figure shown in option (a) having extra circle, option (b) having closed arrow and option (c) having one missing arrow.

Option (d) is similar to the question figure.

Hence, option (d) is correct answer.

EXAMPLE 2 Which object is exactly same as the given figure?

 (a)  (b)  (c)  (d) 

Sol. *(d)* Option (d) is exactly same as question figure.

From the above example we conclude that "Find Similar Shapes" means two figure are said to be similar if they are same in shape and size.

The following steps can help the students to find the answer.

Step 1 : Look at the question figure carefully.

Step 2 : Find the question figure exactly in answer figure which is same in shape and size.

Step 3 : Ignore the remaining option and mark your correct answer.

Let's Practice

Directions (Q. Nos. 1-20) Which object is same as the given figure?

1. (a) (b) (c) (d)

2. (a) (b) (c) (d)

3. (a) (b) (c) (d)

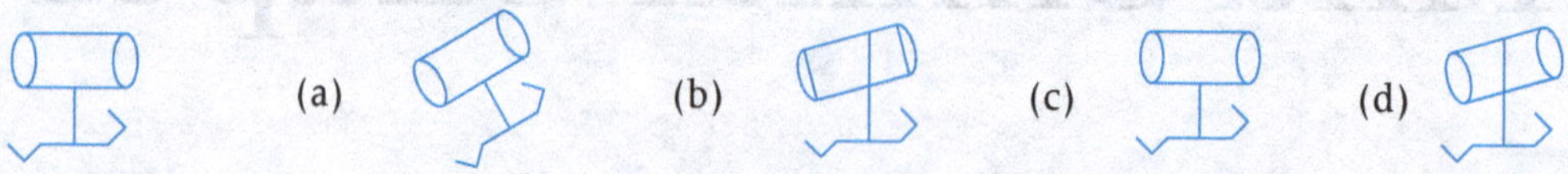

4. (a) (b) (c) (d)

5. (a) (b) (c) (d)

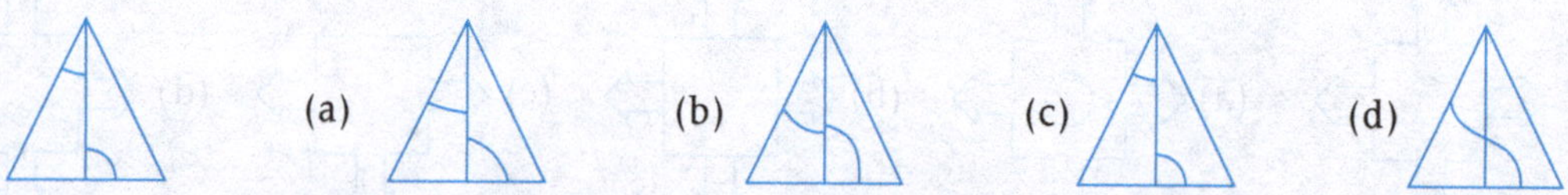

6. (a) (b) (c) (d)

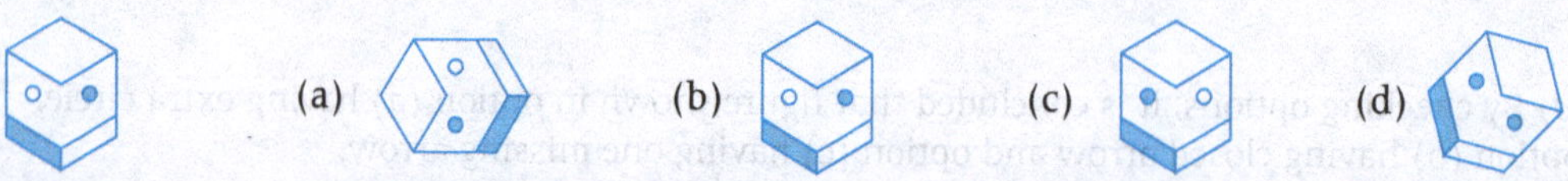

7. (a) (b) (c) (d)

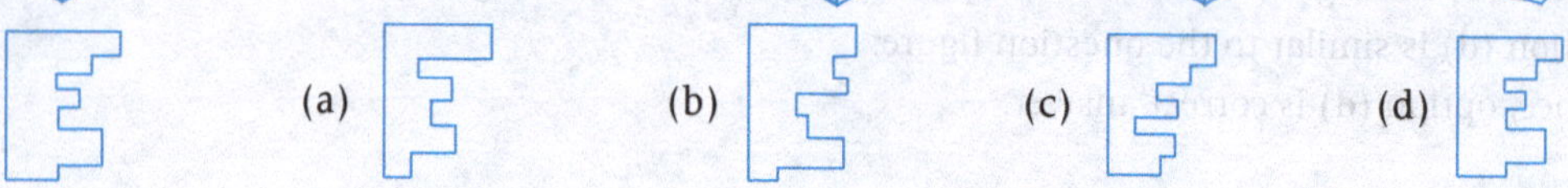

8. (a) (b) (c) (d)

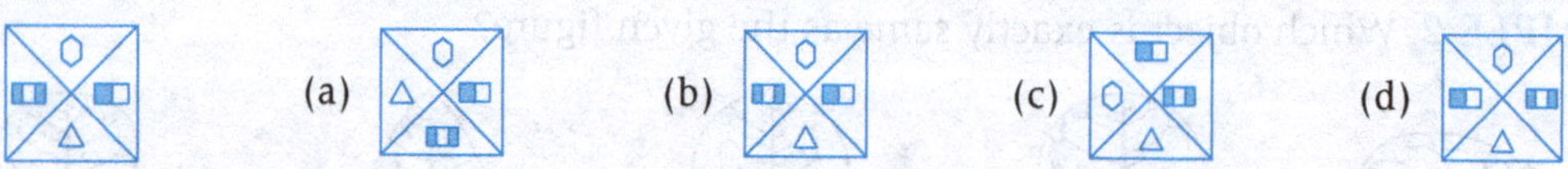

9. (a) (b) (c) (d)

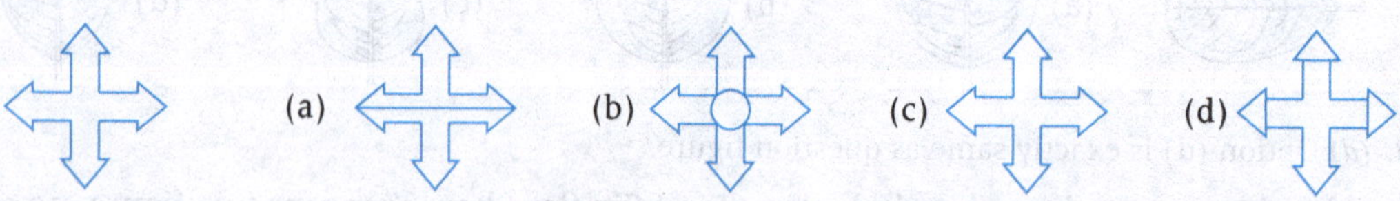

10. (a) (b) (c) (d)

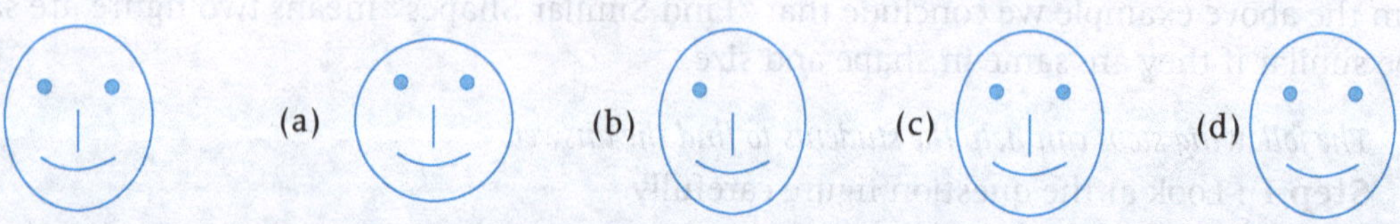

11. 
(a) (b) (c) (d)

12. 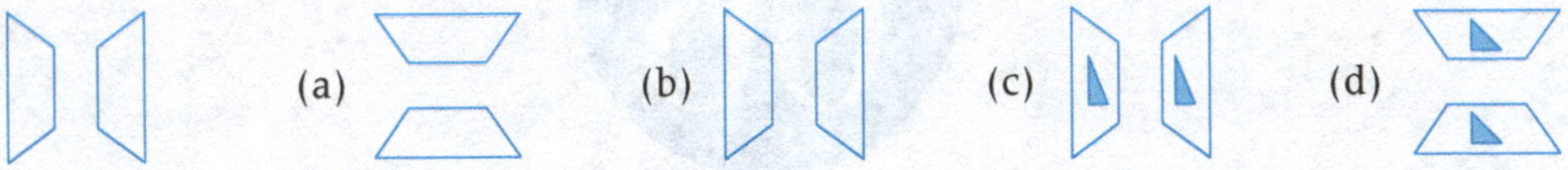
(a) (b) (c) (d)

13. 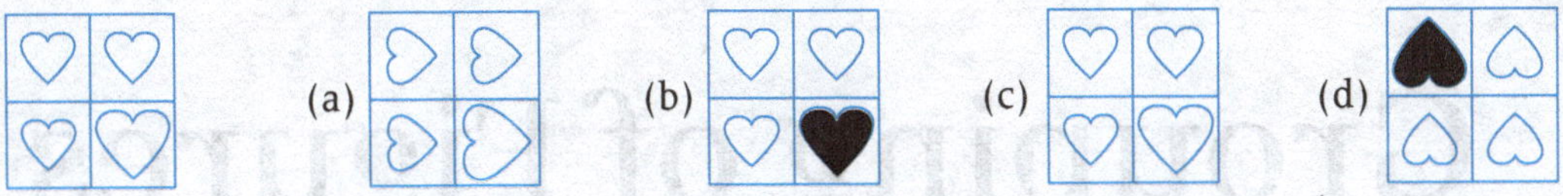
(a) (b) (c) (d)

14. 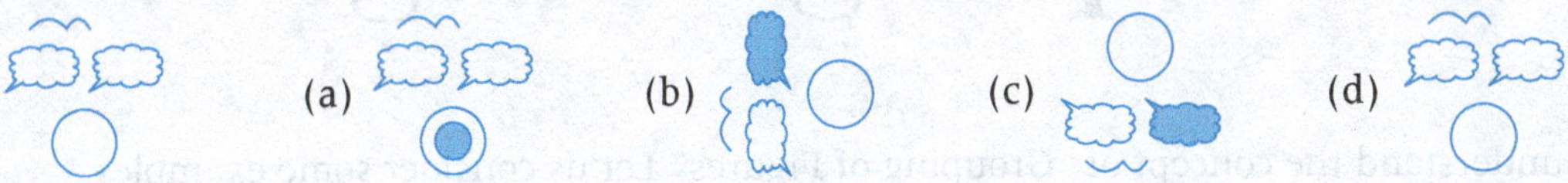
(a) (b) (c) (d)

15. 
(a) (b) (c) (d)

16. 
(a) (b) (c) (d)

17. 
(a) (b) (c) (d)

18. 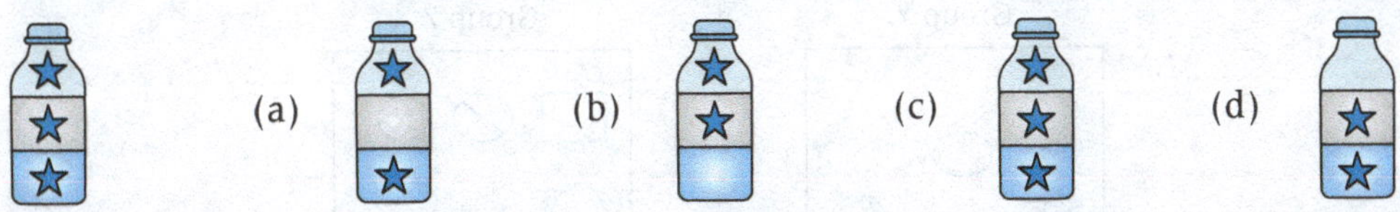
(a) (b) (c) (d)

19. 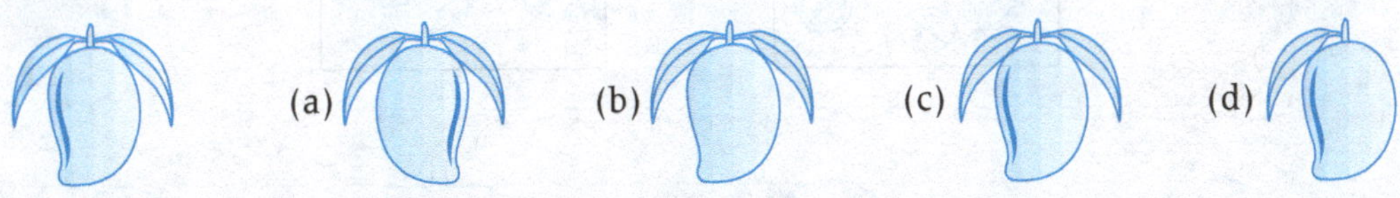
(a) (b) (c) (d)

20. 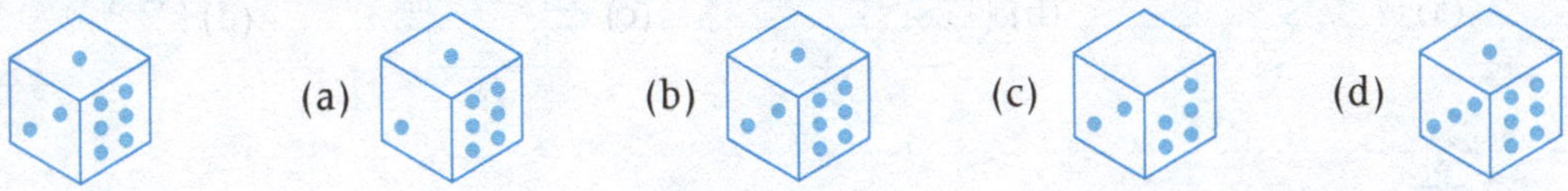
(a) (b) (c) (d)

Chapter 06

Grouping of Figures

To understand the concept of "Grouping of Figures" Let us consider some examples.

EXAMPLE 1

Group X

Which of the given symbol in 'Group X' does not belong to 'Group Y and Z'?

Group Y

Group Z

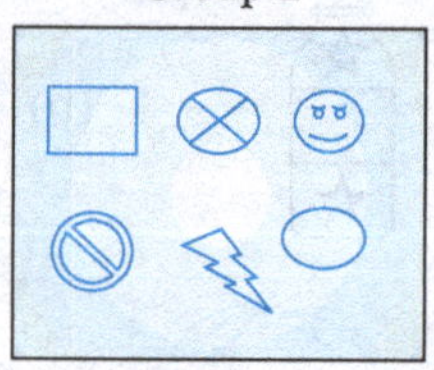

(a)  (b)  (c) 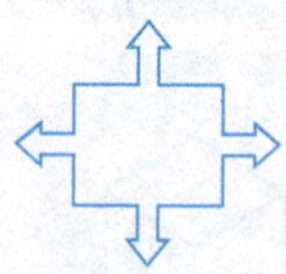 (d) 

Sol. *(c)*  symbol does not belong to Group Y and Z.

Hence, option (c) is correct.

EXAMPLE 2 There are 4 equal groups of .... Football.

(a) 3 (b) 4 (c) 5 (d) 6

Sol. *(b)* There are 4 equal groups of 3 Football.

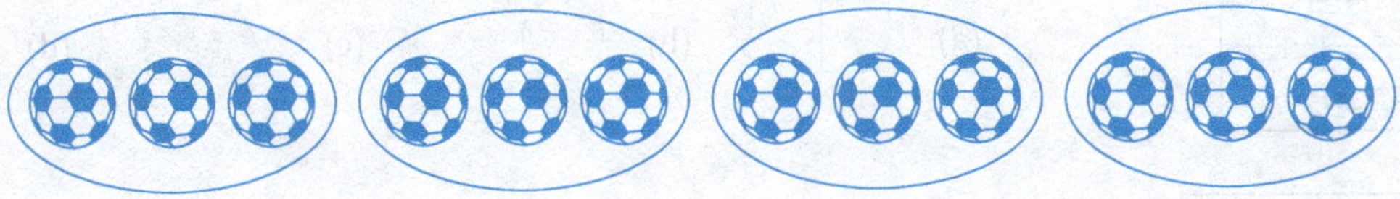

EXAMPLE 3 Count the number of cycles and classify them into groups (Hint 1 group = 2 cycles)

(a) 1 (b) 2 (c) 3 (d) 4

Sol. *(c)* There are 6 cycles in the given figure. As we have given, 1 group = 2 cycles.

So, the number of groups of 6 cycles have = 3 groups.

Hence, option (c) is correct.

"Grouping of Figures" can be done on the basis of their shape, size and figures and classify them into different groups on the basis of their characteristics.

The following steps can help you to solving the questions.

Step 1 : Analyse the given set of Pictures/Figures.

Step 2 : Classify them into groups according to the requirement of question.

Step 3 : Find the option which as is suitable for Question.

Let's Practice

Directions (Q. Nos. 1-5) Identify the object that belongs to the given group.

1. 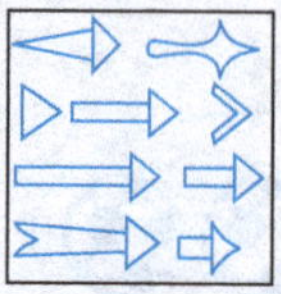

(a)  (b)  (c)  (d) 

2. 

(a)  (b)  (c)  (d) 

3. 

(a)  (b)  (c)  (d) 

4. 

(a)  (b)  (c)  (d) 

5. The given figure  belongs to which group ?

(a)  (b) 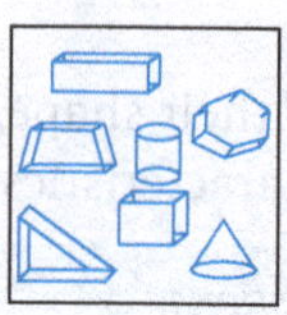 (c)  (d) 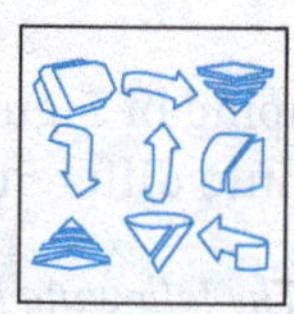

6. There are .... groups of 3 flowers.

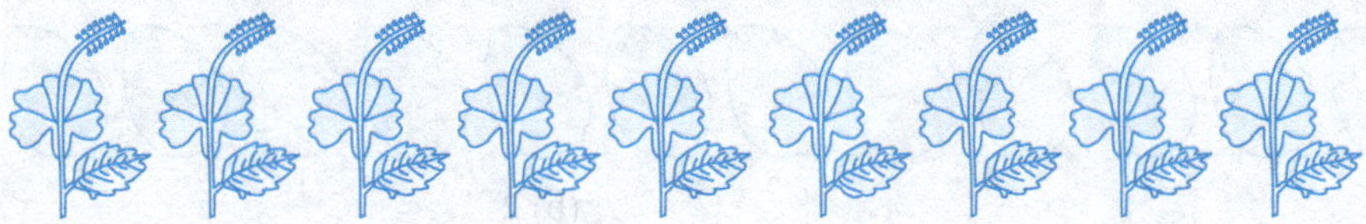

(a) 5 (b) 9 (c) 3 (d) 6

7. There are .... equal groups of 5 triangles.

(a) 7 (b) 5 (c) 3 (d) 6

8. Number of the groups of 6 straws shown here is ....

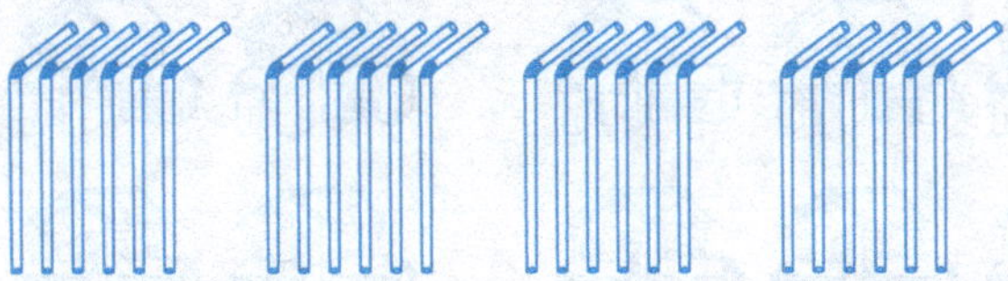

(a) 5 (b) 4
(c) 8 (d) 6

9. There are .... equal groups of 2 horse each.

(a) 8 (b) 10 (c) 5 (d) 14

10. There are .... equal groups of 5.

(a) 5 (b) 10 (c) 7 (d) 4

11. There are .... group of 4 eggs.

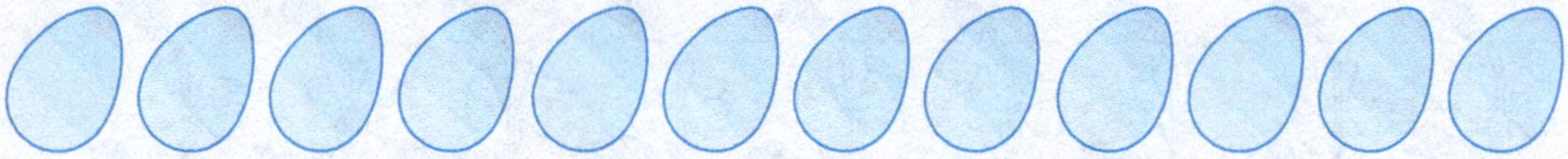

(a) 1
(b) 2
(c) 3
(d) 4

12. Number of the groups 5 balloons shown here is

(a) 1
(b) 2
(c) 3
(d) 4

13. There are .... House in each groups.

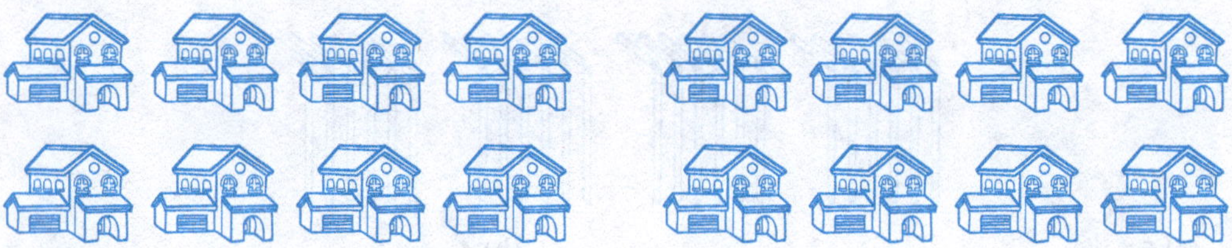

(a) 4
(b) 10
(c) 7
(d) 6

Directions (Q. Nos. 14 and 15) Identify the object that belongs to the group.

14. Identify the object that belongs to the group

(a) 
(b) 
(c) 
(d) 

15.

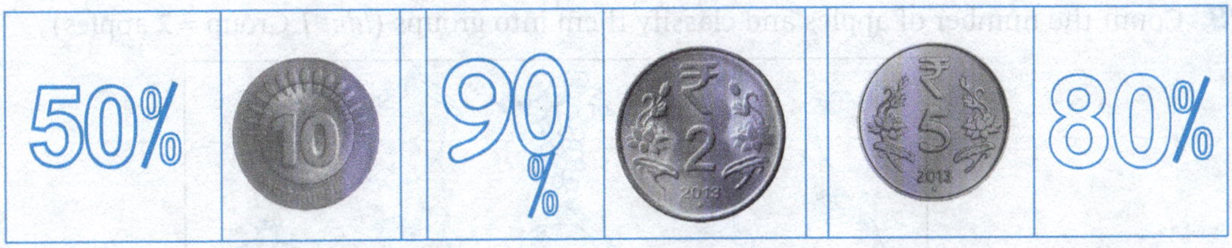

(Group I) (Group II) (Group III)

(a)

(b)

(c)

(d)

Direction (Q. No. 16) The object figures A and B are different from each other by ... .

16.

A

B

(a) Shape
(b) Size
(c) Quantity
(d) Shape and Size

17. The given figure  belongs to group

Group X

Group Y

Group Z

(a) X and Y
(b) Z and Y
(c) X and Z
(d) X and Y

18. Count the number of apples and classify them into groups (*hint 1* Group = 2 apples)

(a) 6 (b) 4 (c) 3 (d) 5

Directions (Q.Nos. 19-21) Study the following diagram carefully and answer the given questions.

19. How many carrots are present in the diagram?

(a) 5 (b) 6 (c) 8 (d) 7

20. How many brinjals are less than peas in the diagram?

(a) 2 (b) 3 (c) 4 (d) 5

21. How many tomatoes are more than cauliflower?

(a) 1 (b) 2 (c) 3 (d) 4

Chapter 07

Hidden Figures

To understand the concept of "Hidden Figure" Let us see some examples.

Directions (Ex. Nos. 1 and 2) Observe the figure and answer the questions below it.

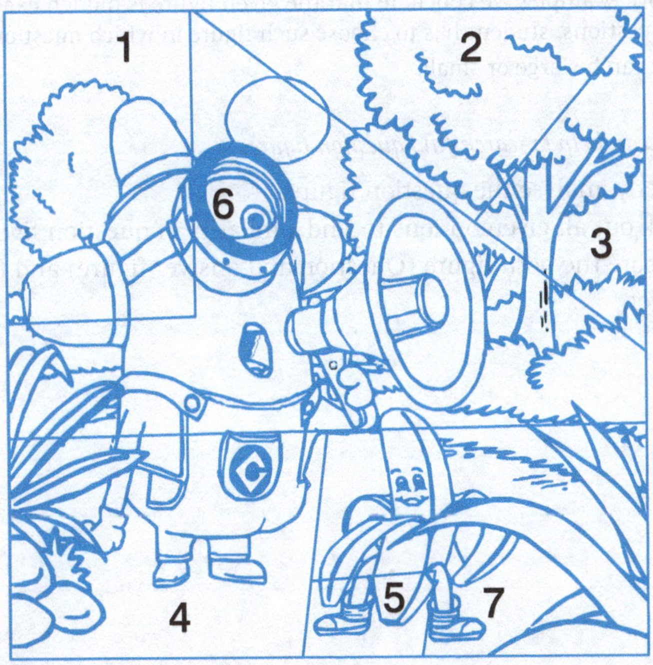

EXAMPLE 1 In which part of the figure is the shape  hidden?

(a) 2 (b) 6 (c) 3 (d) 5

Sol. *(b)* The shape given in the question is hidden in part 6.
Hence, option (b) is correct.

EXAMPLE 2 Which shape is hidden in part 7?

(a)  (b)  (c)  (d) 

Sol. *(a)* Shape of option (a) is hidden in part 7.

Example 3 Which larger shape has the shape  hidden in it ?

(a)  (b)  (c)  (d) 

Sol. *(c)* From the above examples we conclude that the given figure is hidden exactly in answer option. In this type of questions, student has to choose such figure in which question figure is hidden. Question Figure can be large or small.

The following steps can help to search/find question figure.

Step 1 : Properly analyse the question figure.

Step 2 : Check out all given options to find similarity of question figure.

Step 3 : Compare the both figure (Question and answer figure) and finally mark your answer.

Let's Practice

Directions (Q. Nos. 1-3) Observe the figure and answer the questions below it.

1. Which shape is hidden in part 3?

(a) 

(b) 

(c) 

(d) 

2. In which part of the figure is the shape  hidden?

(a) 3 (b) 7 (c) 1 (d) 5

3. How many of the pictures given in the box are hidden in the part 7?

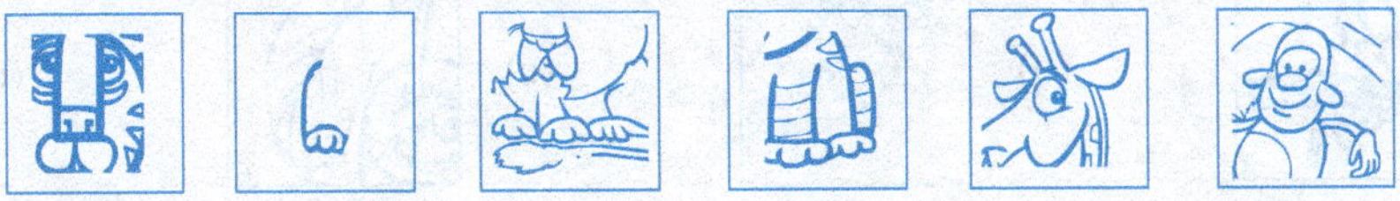

(a) 4 (b) 6 (c) 1 (d) 2

Directions (Q. Nos. 4-7) Observe the figure and answer the question below it.

4. How many eyes are there in part 4?

(a) 12 (b) 10 (c) 4 (d) 8

5. In which part of the figure is the shape  hidden?

(a) 3 (b) 6 (c) 1 (d) 4

6. Which of the following shape is hidden in part 3?

(a)  (b)  (c)  (d) 

7. How many stands  are there in part 7 ?

(a) 5 (b) 4 (c) 2 (d) 1

8. In which shape has the shape  hidden ?

(a) 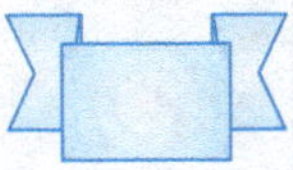 (b) 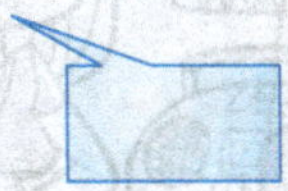 (c)  (d) 

9. Which has the shape  hidden in it ?

(a)  (b)  (c)  (d) 

10. Which larger shape has the shape  hidden in it ?

(a)  (b)  (c)  (d) 

11. Which larger shape has the shape  hidden in it ?

(a)  (b)  (c)  (d) 

12. Which larger shape has the shape  hidden in it ?

(a)  (b)  (c) 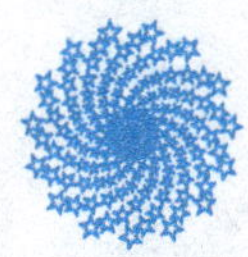 (d) 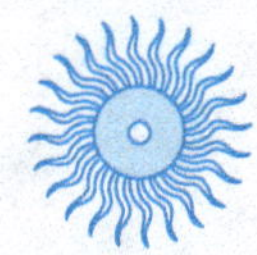

Directions (Q. Nos. 13 and 14) Observe the figure and answer the question below it.

13. In which part of the figure is the shape  hidden?

(a) 2 (b) 6 (c) 1 (d) 4

14. Which shape is hidden in part 4 ?

(a)  (b)  (c) 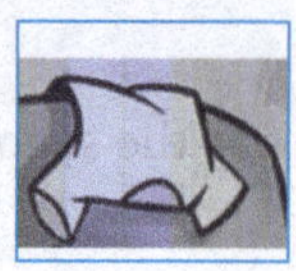 (d) 

Chapter

08

Position Test

To understand the concept of "Ranking Test" Let us see some examples.

EXAMPLE 1. Which Sun is 5th from the right end?

Left and → ← Right end

(a) U (b) R (c) T (d) X

Sol. *(c)* Sun T is fifth from right end.

Hence, option (c) is correct.

Example 2 The third letter from the right end in the given month is?

F E B R U A R Y

(a) R (b) A (c) U (d) B

Sol. *(b)* A is third from the right end.

Hence, option (b) is correct.

From the above examples we conclude that "Ranking Test" means arrangement of Position or ranks of an object or a person either from Left to Right or top to bottom.

The following step can help you to find the answer.

Step 1 : What is ask in the question (which type) Identify first carefully.

Step 2 : Top and Bottom to be count as per requirement. Left and Right to be selected from our Left end and Right end.

Step 3 : Solve them accordingly step 2 requirement and mark your correct answer.

Let's Practice

1. The fourth letter from the right end is __________.

E K Z H L W B N Y

(a) T (b) K (c) H (d) W

2. Subtract the 2nd number from the right end from the 5th number from the right end and you will get the _______ number from left end.

5 3 1 4 2 8

(a) 2nd (b) 1st
(c) 4th (d) 3rd

3. Add the 1st number from the left to the 4th number from the left end and you will get the _______ number from right end.

3 2 6 4 1 7 5

(a) 3rd (b) 2nd
(c) 6th (d) 4th

4. If there is no 'L' in the given word, then Y is the ______ letter from the left end.

P L A Y I N G

(a) 3rd (b) 2nd
(c) 1st (d) 4th

5. Which monkey is fifth from the left end?

F K T P A O G I Z

(a) E (b) H
(c) A (d) F

6. Which image is 3rd from the right end?

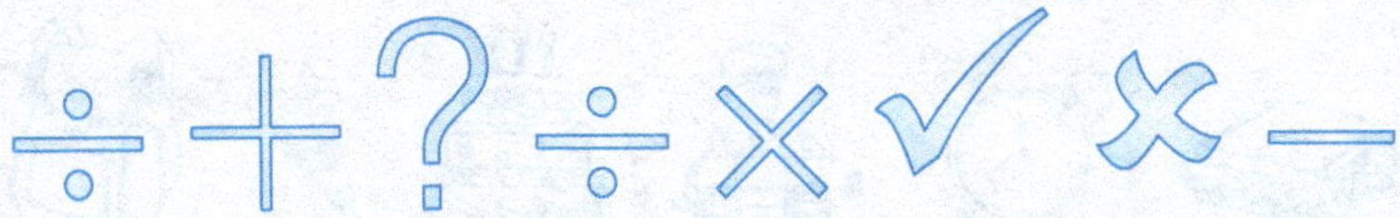

(a)  (b) 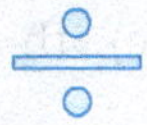 (c)  (d) 

7. Which cap is 7th from the left end?

A M G P F X C L B N Z

(a) C (b) H (c) D (d) J

8. Which fruit basket is 8th from the right end?

L M N O P Q R S

(a) L (b) D (c) M (d) F

9. The position of the circle is __________ .

(a) 3rd from the right end (b) 3rd from the left end
(c) 5th from the left end (d) 5th from the right end

10. The position of arrow is ....?

(a) 2nd from the left end (b) 4th from the left end
(c) 2nd from the right end (d) 6th from right end

11. If there is no mango in the picture, then the apple is now the _________ item from the right end.

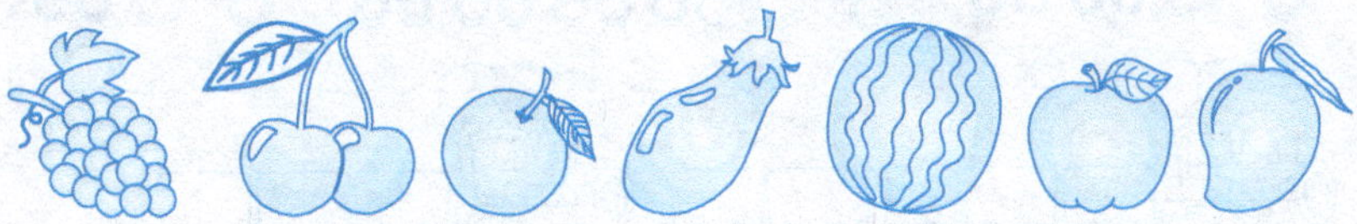

(a) 4th (b) 6th (c) 1st (d) 3rd

12. If there is no car in the picture, then the cake is now the ________ item from the left end.

(a) 3rd (b) 4th (c) 5th (d) 6th

13. If we destroy the house no. 4 then the position of house no. 7 is now from the left end is?

House no.1 House no.2 House no.3 House no.4 House no.5 House no.6 House no.7 House no.8 House no.9 House no.10

(a) 2nd (b) 4th (c) 5th (d) 6th

14. The position of encircled car is ____________ .

(a) 1st from the right end
(b) 3rd from the left end
(c) 6th from the right end
(d) 5th from the left end

15. In the given sequence which of the following person is thinking something?

(a) 2nd from the left end person
(b) 4th from the left end person
(c) 6th from the right end person
(d) 3rd from right end person

16. The position of train having 2 bogey is ____________ .

(a) 2nd from the left end
(b) 1st from the left end
(c) 2nd from the right end
(d) 1st from the right end

Directions (Q. Nos. 17 and 18) On the basis of following figure, fill in the blanks.

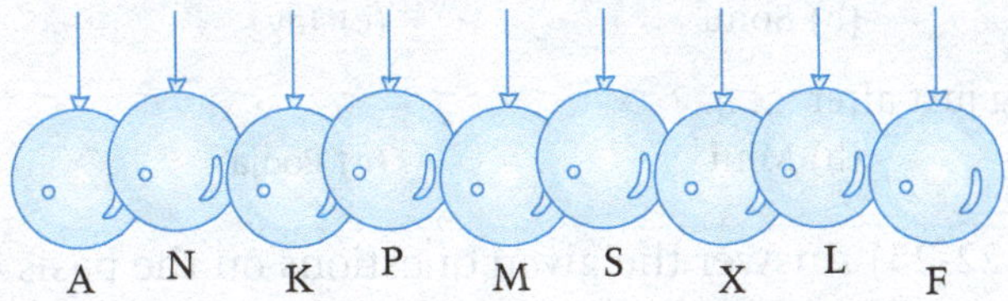

17. Balloon M is between _________ .

(a) balloon K and balloon X
(b) balloon P and balloon S
(c) balloon A and balloon F
(d) balloon A and balloon K

18. First balloon from the left end and first balloon from the right end are _________ .

(a) balloon A and balloon M
(b) balloon K and balloon A
(c) balloon M and balloon F
(d) balloon A and balloon F

Directions (Q. Nos.19-21) Answer of the given question on the basis of the following figure.

19. Pooja is in between .... and ......?

(a) Jay and Sonu
(b) Sunny and Jay
(c) Mini and Jay
(d) Sonu and Mini

20. Who is climbing on the top.

(a) Mini (b) Sonu (c) Jay (d) Pooja

21. Sunny is climbing just after .... ?

(a) Jay (b) Mini (c) Pooja (d) Sonu

Directions (Q. Nos. 22-25) Answer the given questions on the basis of following figure.

22. Mahima is between ________ .

(a) Mohan and Ramesh (b) Pankaj and Gitika
(c) Ramesh and Gitika (d) Pooja and Rohan

23. Who is third in the row?

(a) Pankaj (b) Mahima
(c) Gitika (d) Ramesh

24. How many children are there in the row?

(a) 8 (b) 4 (c) 9 (d) 5

25. Pooja is just after ________ .

(a) Rohan (b) Mahima
(c) Shalu (d) Gitika

PRACTICE SET 01

1. What comes next?

 ?

(a)  (b)  (c)  (d) 

2. The given figure  belongs to which group?

P Q R S

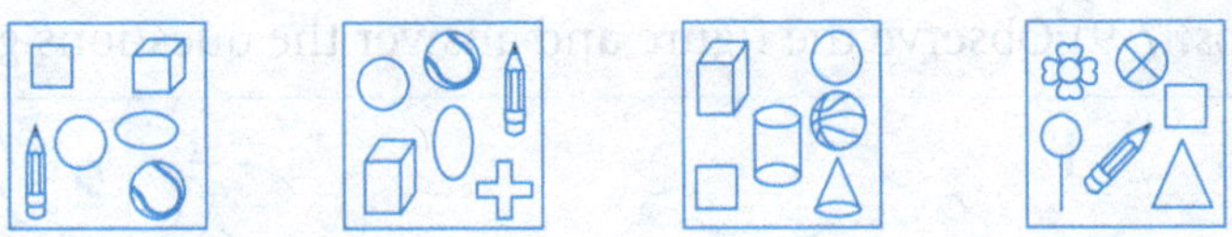

(a) R (b) Q (c) P (d) S

3. The position of car having 1 boy is __________ .

(a) 3rd from the right end
(b) 4th from the right end
(c) 2nd from the left end
(d) 5th from the left end

4. In which larger shape is the shape  hidden?

(a)  (b)  (c)  (d) 

5. Which figure is exactly same as the given figure?

(a)  (b)  (c)  (d) 

6. Which alphabet is 6th from the right end?

R V J E Y O M T C

(a) Y (b) V (c) E (d) J

Directions (Q. Nos. 7-9) Observe the figure and answer the questions given below.

7. In which part of the figure is the shape  hidden?

(a) 4 (b) 3
(c) 2 (d) 5

8. Which shape is hidden in part 7?

(a) 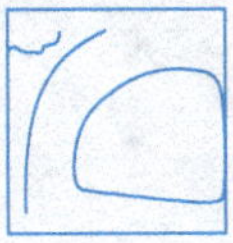 (b)  (c)  (d) 

9. How many of the pictures given in the box are hidden in the part 3?

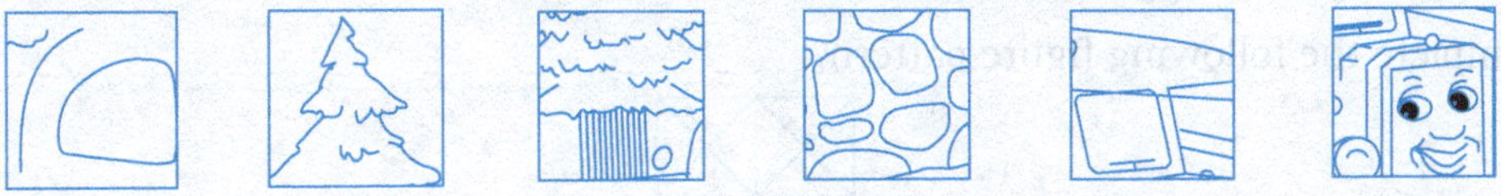

(a) 1 (b) 2
(c) 5 (d) 3

10. Which one is different from others?

(a)  (b)  (c)  (d) 

11. Which one comes next?

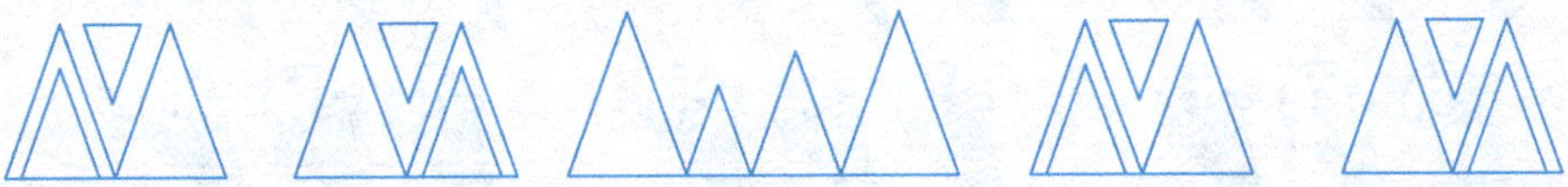 ?

(a)  (b) 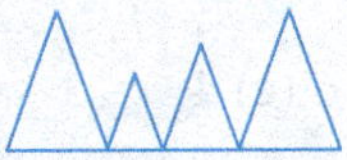 (c)  (d) 

12. Which one is different from others?

(a)  (b) 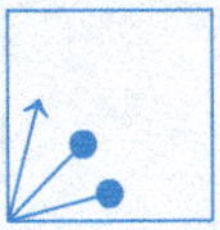 (c) 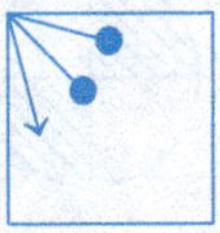 (d) 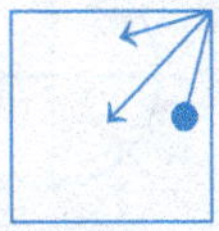

13. If there is no triangle in the given figure, then the circle is the .... item from the left end.

(a) 4th (b) 6th (c) 3rd (d) 2nd

14. Choose the correct option.

D E/C : CDE :: N O/M ?

(a) NMC (b) MNO (c) MXL (d) ABC

15. Complete the following figure pattern.

(a) 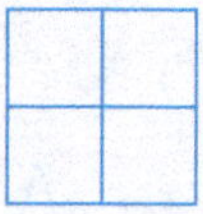 (b)  (c)  (d) 

16. How many groups of 3 cones can be formed from the following figures?

(a) 8 (b) 5 (c) 4 (d) 6

17. Complete the second pair in the same way as first pair.

(a) 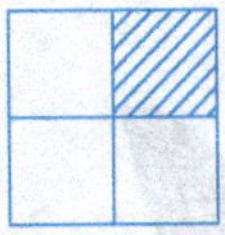 (b) 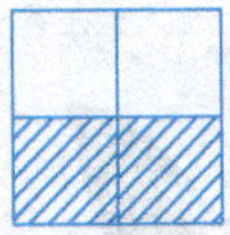 (c) 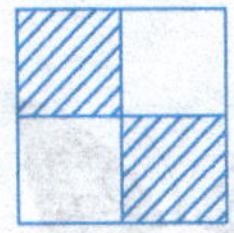 (d) 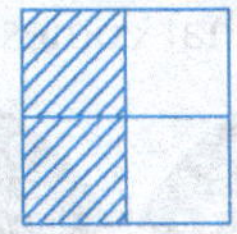

18. Which figure is different from others?

(a)  (b)  (c)  (d) 

19. Which letter is third from the left end in the word given below?

SOLUTION

(a) U
(b) O
(c) T
(d) L

20. Complete the second pair in the same way as the first pair.

(a)  (b)  (c)  (d) 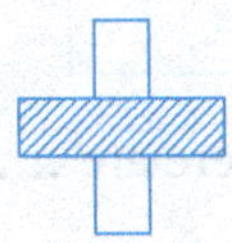

21. Choose the correct option.

Six : 6 :: Seven : ?

(a) 8
(b) Five
(c) 7
(d) Nine

22. What comes next?

(a) 47
(b) 45
(c) 42
(d) 50

23. Find the other half of the given picture from the options provided.

(a) 

(b) 

(c) 

(d) 

24. Which object is same as the given figure?

(a) 

(b) 

(c) 

(d) 

25. There are .... equal groups of 6 glass of juice.

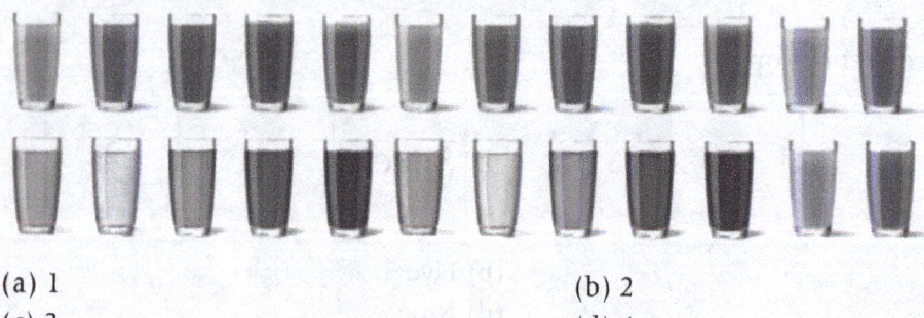

(a) 1
(b) 2
(c) 3
(d) 4

26. Which has the shape  hidden in it?

(a)  (b) 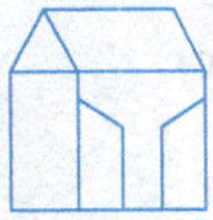 (c)  (d) 

27. Which is the 4th letter from the left end in the given word?

COMPUTER

(a) T (b) R (c) O (d) P

28. Find the missing figure?

(a)  (b)  (c)  (d) 

29. Complete the given number figure.

(a)  (b)  (c)  (d) 

30. Which object is same as the given figure?

(a)  (b)  (c)  (d) 

31. Identify the object that belongs to the group.

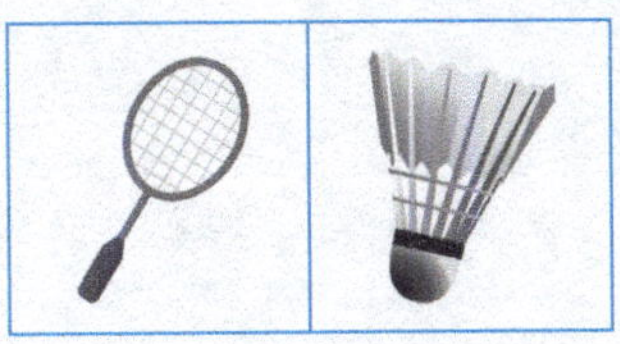

(Group I)

(Group II)

(Group III)

(a) 
(b) 
(c) 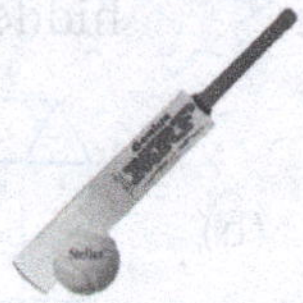
(d) 

32. What comes next?

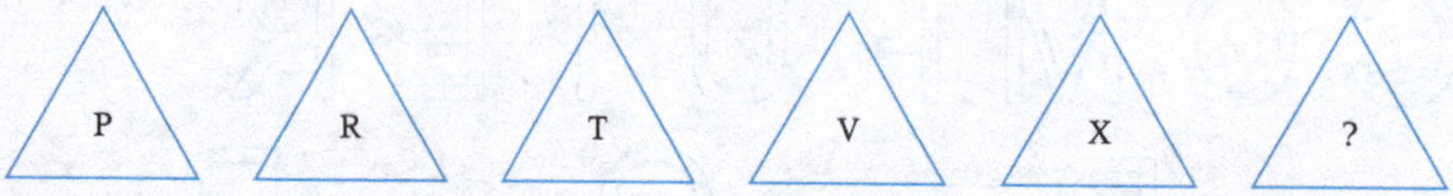

(a) U
(b) S
(c) M
(d) Z

33. Find the other half of the given word?

(a) 
(b) 
(c) et
(d) te

34. Which shape is hidden in the question figure?

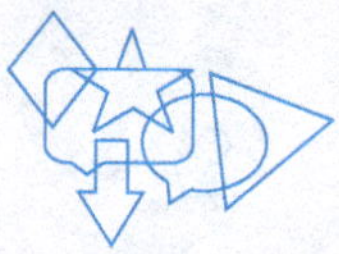

(a) 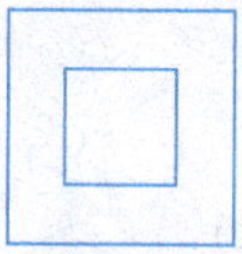
(b) 
(c) 
(d) 

35. What is the position of Evan?

(a) 1st
(b) 2nd
(c) 3rd
(d) 4th

PRACTICE SET 02

1. Complete the second pair in the same way as the first pair.

 : 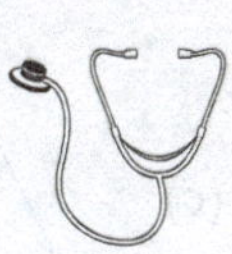 ::  : ?

(a) 
(b) 
(c) 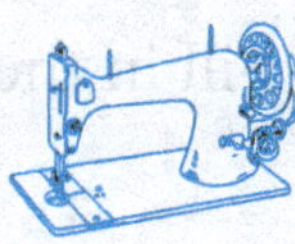
(d) 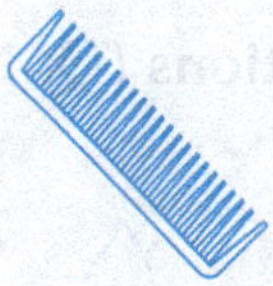

2. Which one comes next?

February	March	April	May	June	July	?

(a) December
(b) August
(c) October
(d) November

3. Which object is same as the given figure?

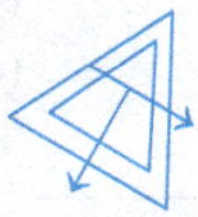

(a) 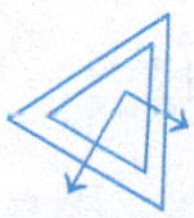
(b) 
(c) 
(d) 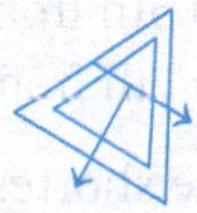

4. Which one is different from others?

(a) 

(b) 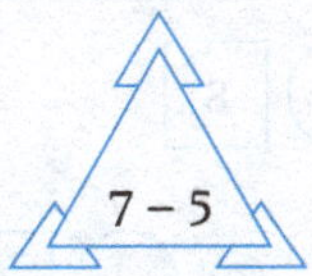

(c) 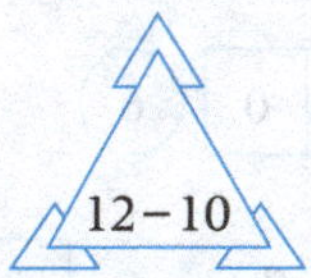

(d) 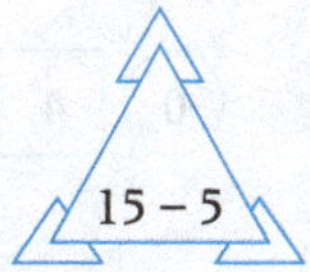

5. Find the missing figure.

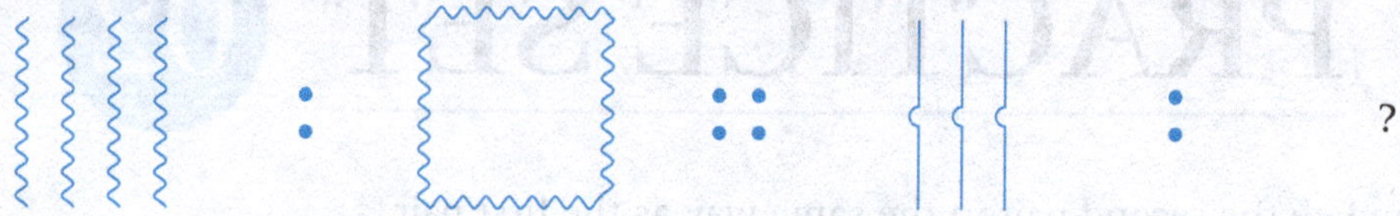

(a) 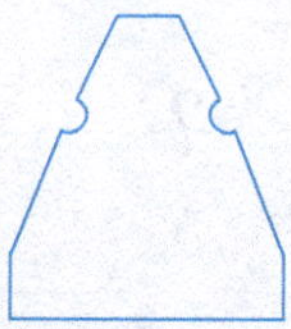 (b)  (c) 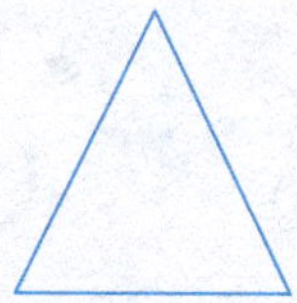 (d) 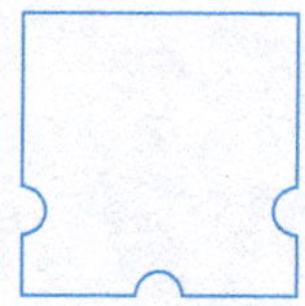

Directions (Q. Nos. 6-8) Fill in the blanks on the basis of given figure.

P J B X K L D M R T V A H

6. Candle K is between ________ .

(a) candle J and candle D
(b) candle R and candle V
(c) candle X and candle L
(d) candle B and candle L

7. The position of shortest candle is ________ .

(a) 5th from the right end
(b) 5th from the left end
(c) 7th from the left end
(d) 7th from the right end

8. The shortest and longest candles are ________ .

(a) K and A
(b) M and B
(c) K and T
(d) H and K

9. Which one comes next?

(a)  (b)  (c)  (d) 

10. The shape  belongs to which of the following groups?

(A)  (B) 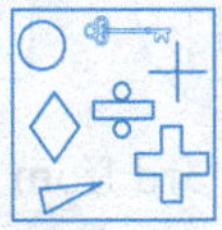 (C)  (D) 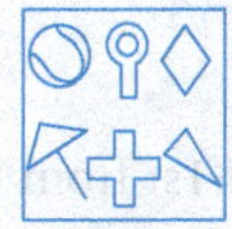

(a) B and D (b) A and C (c) A and D (d) C and D

11. Which figure is same as the given figure?

(a)  (b)  (c)  (d) 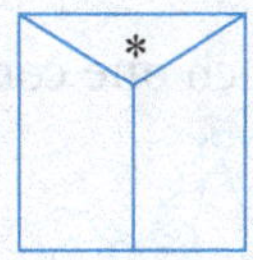

12. Find the other half of the picture given below.

(a)  (b)  (c)  (d) 

13. Find the missing figure.

USN :  :: THA : ?

(a) 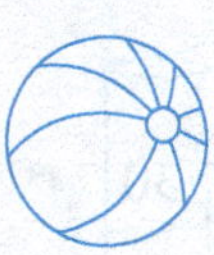 (b)  (c)  (d) 

14. The position of number in the circle is _________ .

(a) 1st from the right end (b) 3rd from the left end
(c) 6th from the right end (d) 5th from the left end

15. The position  from the right end is ______.

(a) 5th (b) 4th (c) 6th (d) 3rd

16. Which one comes next?

(a) 

(b) 

(c) 

(d) 

17. In which larger shape is the shape  hidden?

(a) 
(b) 
(c) 
(d) 

18. Which one is different from others?

(a) 

(b) 

(c) 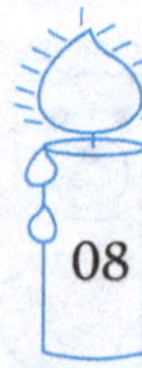

(d) 

19. Which option will replace the question mark?

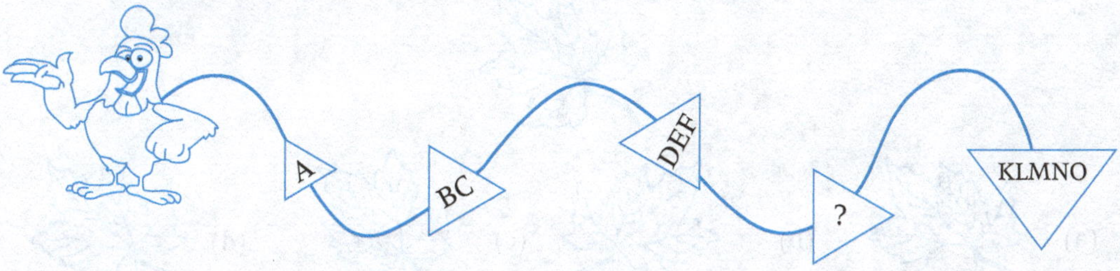

(a) GHIJ (b) POR (c) EFGH (d) BCD

20. Choose the figure which will complete the given figure pattern.

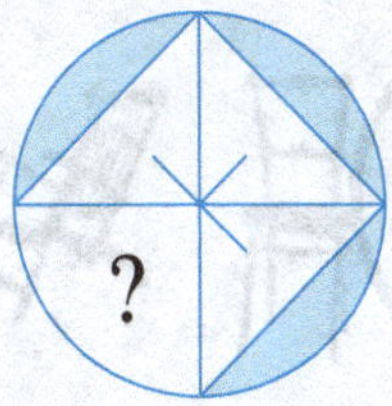

(a)  (b)  (c) 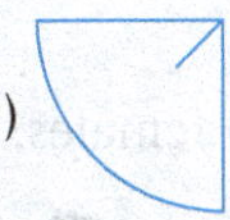 (d) 

21. If 8 is related to 800, then 9 is related to .... ?

(a) 1000 (b) 700 (c) 90 (d) 900

22. Which one is different from others?

(a)  (b)  (c)  (d) 

23. Which will complete the given figure?

(a)  (b)  (c)  (d) 

24. Which object is same as the given figure?

(a)  (b)  (c)  (d) 

25. The position of encircled chair is .... from left end.

(a) 1st (b) 2nd (c) 3rd (d) 4th

26. There are .... group of 3 females.

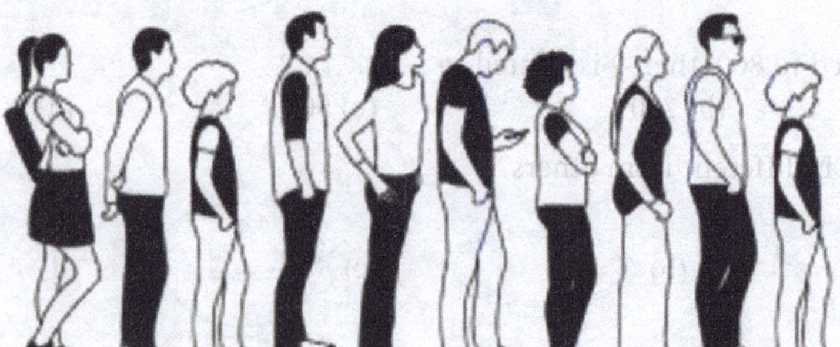

(a) 1 (b) 2 (c) 3 (d) 4

27. Which object is same as the given figure?

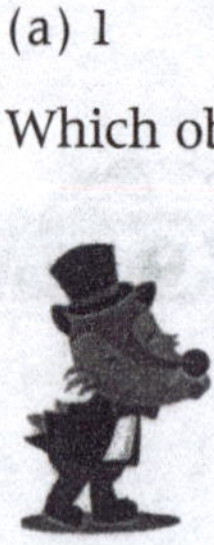 (a) 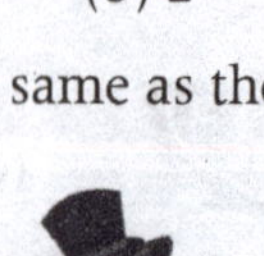 (b) 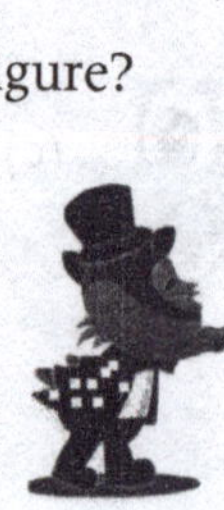 (c) 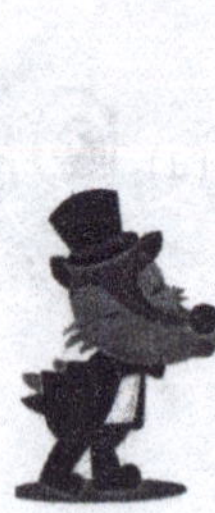 (d) 

28. The objects in figures A and B are different from each other by ....

(A)

(B)

(a) Shape (b) Size (c) Quantity (d) Shape and size

Directions (Q. Nos. 29-31) Observe the figure and answer the questions below it?

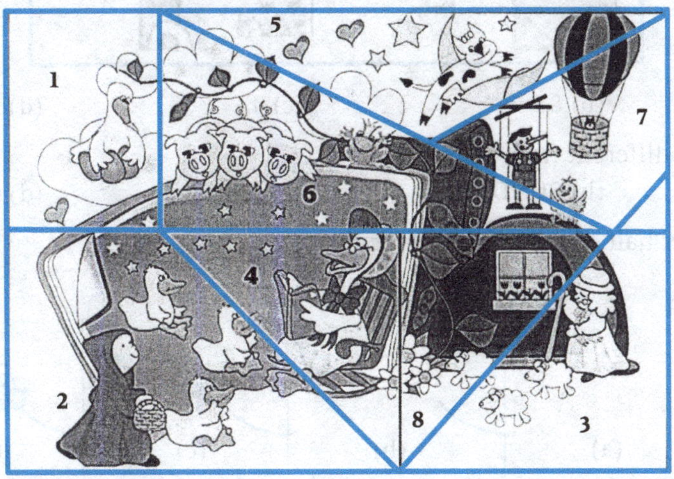

29. Which shape is hidden in part 7 ?

(a)  (b)  (c)  (d) 

30. In which part of figure is the shape hidden?

(a) 2 (b) 4 (c) 6 (d) 8

31. How many of the pictures given in the box are hidden in the part '8'?

(a) 2 (b) 8 (c) 4 (d) 5

32. Which one is different from others?

(a) MAY (b) SUNDAY (c) JUNE (d) OCTOBER

33. Find the other half of the given number?

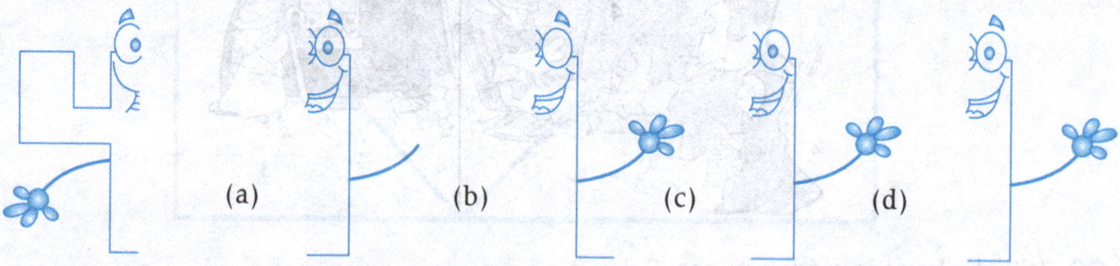

34. Who is standing in the middle of the queue?

(a) Ram (b) Siya (c) Deepa (d) Pari

35. Observe the figure and answer the question below it.

How many fish are in the given figure?

(a) 2 (b) 4

(c) 5 (d) 6

Answers

1. Matching Pairs

1. (c)	2. (b)	3. (b)	4. (a)	5. (d)	6. (c)	7. (c)	8. (b)	9. (b)	10. (c)
11. (d)	12. (c)	13. (b)	14. (b)	15. (c)	16. (c)	17. (a)	18. (b)	19. (a)	20. (c)
21. (b)	22. (b)	23. (b)	24. (a)	25. (d)	26. (d)	27. (d)	28. (c)	29. (d)	30. (b)

2. Odd One Out

1. (d)	2. (a)	3. (c)	4. (d)	5. (d)	6. (d)	7. (d)	8. (c)	9. (d)	10. (d)
11. (c)	12. (d)	13. (c)	14. (c)	15. (b)	16. (b)	17. (c)	18. (b)	19. (d)	20. (c)
21. (b)	22. (c)	23. (c)	24. (a)	25. (d)					

3. What Comes Next?

1. (c)	2. (d)	3. (b)	4. (c)	5. (b)	6. (d)	7. (b)	8. (d)	9. (b)	10. (c)
11. (b)	12. (c)	13. (d)	14. (b)	15. (c)	16. (d)	17. (c)	18. (b)	19. (c)	20. (c)
21. (c)	22. (c)	23. (b)	24. (c)	25. (b)					

4. Complete the Figures

1. (c)	2. (c)	3. (c)	4. (a)	5. (d)	6. (a)	7. (d)	8. (c)	9. (b)	10. (b)
11. (d)	12. (c)	13. (a)	14. (d)	15. (b)	16. (c)	17. (b)	18. (a)	19. (d)	20. (b)
21. (a)	22. (d)	23. (d)							

5. Find Similar Shapes

1. (d)	2. (c)	3. (c)	4. (b)	5. (c)	6. (b)	7. (d)	8. (b)	9. (c)	10. (c)
11. (a)	12. (b)	13. (c)	14. (d)	15. (b)	16. (a)	17. (b)	18. (c)	19. (c)	20. (b)

6. Grouping of Figures

1. (c)	2. (d)	3. (c)	4. (b)	5. (c)	6. (c)	7. (b)	8. (b)	9. (b)	10. (d)
11. (c)	12. (c)	13. (a)	14. (a)	15. (a)	16. (d)	17. (c)	18. (c)	19. (d)	20. (a)
21. (a)									

7. Hidden Figures

1. (a)	2. (b)	3. (d)	4. (b)	5. (b)	6. (b)	7. (c)	8. (d)	9. (d)	10. (c)
11. (b)	12. (a)	13. (b)	14. (d)						

8. Position Test

1. (d)	2. (d)	3. (b)	4. (a)	5. (c)	6. (c)	7. (a)	8. (a)	9. (b)	10. (b)
11. (c)	12. (a)	13. (d)	14. (d)	15. (d)	16. (b)	17. (b)	18. (d)	19. (b)	20. (a)
21. (b)	22. (d)	23. (c)	24. (d)	25. (d)					

Practice Set 1

1. (b)	2. (a)	3. (b)	4. (d)	5. (d)	6. (c)	7. (d)	8. (d)	9. (b)	10. (b)
11. (b)	12. (d)	13. (a)	14. (b)	15. (d)	16. (d)	17. (c)	18. (d)	19. (d)	20. (a)
21. (c)	22. (b)	23. (b)	24. (b)	25. (d)	26. (c)	27. (d)	28. (b)	29. (c)	30. (c)
31. (c)	32. (d)	33. (d)	34. (c)	35. (d)					

Practice Set 2

1. (c)	2. (b)	3. (d)	4. (d)	5. (b)	6. (c)	7. (b)	8. (c)	9. (b)	10. (a)
11. (d)	12. (b)	13. (d)	14. (d)	15. (c)	16. (c)	17. (a)	18. (c)	19. (a)	20. (b)
21. (d)	22. (d)	23. (a)	24. (d)	25. (d)	26. (b)	27. (c)	28. (c)	29. (c)	30. (c)
31. (d)	32. (b)	33. (d)	34. (c)	35. (c)					

Hints & Solutions

Matching Pairs

1. (c) As, there are 3 letters present in first word. Similarly, there are 4 letters present in second.

2. (b) As,

$M \xrightarrow{+1} N$

$O \longrightarrow O$ (fixed)

$N \xrightarrow{+1} O$

Similarly,

$S \xrightarrow{+1} T$

$O \longrightarrow O$ (fixed)

$N \xrightarrow{+1} O$

3. (b) Second letter is immediate of first letter.

As, $P \xrightarrow{+1} Q$

Similarly, $I \xrightarrow{+1} J$

4. (a) As,

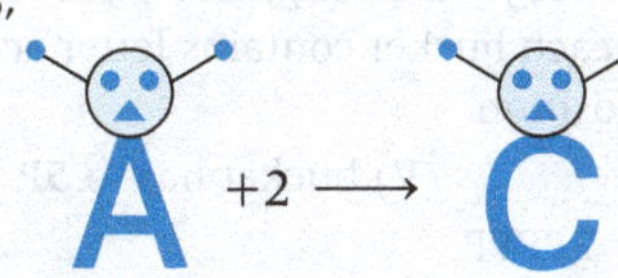

Similarly,

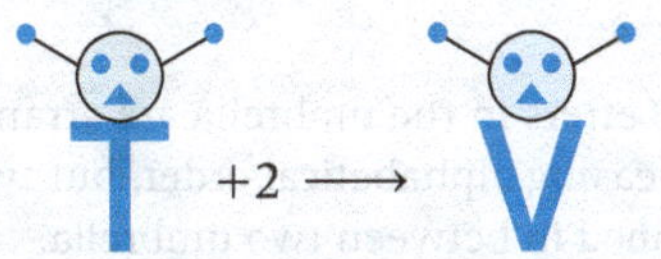

5. (d) As AB are starting alphabets and YZ are last alphabets. In same way CD and WX are third and fourth alphabets from starting and last, respectively.

6. (c) Second figure is the mirror reflection of the first figure.

7. (c) Second figure is the completed figure of the first figure.

8. (b) As, $10 - 1 = 9$

Similarly, $20 - 1 = 19$

9. (b) As, $10 \longrightarrow 100$ (put a zero ahead)

Similarly, $20 \longrightarrow 200$ (put a zero ahead)

10. (c) As, in first figure there are 3 circle present.

Similarly, in second figure there are 4 squares present.

11. (d) As, $55 - 5 = 50$ (Subtraction Rule)

Similarly, $65 - 5 = 60$ (Subtraction Rule)

12. (c) Given number is the total number of petals present in the flower.

13. (b) As, 5 are related to 5 rings. Similarly, 7 are related to 7 boxes.

14. (b) As, $20 \times 2 = 40$

Similarly, $30 \times 2 = 60$

15. (c) Bag is used to put the books. Similarly, flower pot is used to put the flowers.

16. (c) Dots are connected with lines to form a geometrical shape.

17. (a) + or × of first figure will disappear to get second figure.

18. (b) Given lines are use to form the second figure.

19. (a) Shaded area interchanges with white area.

20. (c) Number of objects is equal to the number of the lines in second figure.

21. (b) × or + disappears and the remaining elements are arranged in the square shape.

22. (b) First figure is divided into two parts to form the second figure.

23. (b) Inner shape becomes the outer shape and outer shape becomes the inner shape.

24. (a) Second figure completes the first figure.

25. (d) Single shape turns into double shapes and double shapes turns into single shape.

26. (d) Second figure is the part of the first figure.

27. (d) Number of *zig-zag* lines is increased by two in second figure.

28. (c) Outer small shapes become central shape and central shape becomes outer shapes.

29. (d) As, the figure inside the square is "circle".

Similarly,

In second pair the figure inside the square is 'cone.'

30. *(b)* Second figure is the main source used by the professional in the first figure.

Odd One Out

1. *(d)* Except option (d), All other groups contains first and second letters in uppercase and third letter in lower case.
2. *(a)* Except option (a), all are consonant. While 'A' is vowel.
3. *(c)* Except option (c), all letters are form a consecutive group of letters of English alphabetical series while 'GHJL' is odd group.
4. *(d)* Except option (d), all are the name of colours.
5. *(d)* Except option (d), rest are vowels.
6. *(d)* Except option (d), all other months have 31 days.
7. *(d)* Except option (d), rest are fruits.
8. *(c)* Except option (c), the given group of numbers are given in ascending order while '457' break the order.
9. *(d)* Except option (d), all numbers are divisible by '10'.
10. *(d)* Except option (d), subtraction of both digits is '5'. While [8 – 2 = 6].
11. *(c)* Except option (c), in all other figures only digits are interchange.
12. *(d)* Except option (d), 2nd number is twice the first number.
13. *(c)* All options have 7 triangles except option (c).
14. *(c)* Except figure (c), all other figures have straight lines.
15. *(b)* Except option (b), the base of arrow is same.
16. *(b)* Except option (b), there are only two bottom lines.
17. *(c)* Except option (c), there are two circles and one triangle in all other options.
18. *(b)* All objects are used for cutting, except option (b).
19. *(d)* All objects are the source of light, except option (d).
20. *(c)* Except option (c), designs of options (a), (b) and (d) are made by straight lines.
21. *(b)* All figures have both the hands in same direction except figure (b).
22. *(c)* All options have same addition of numbers i.e. 5, except option (c).
23. *(c)* Except option (c), all other options have two similar shapes.
24. *(a)* Except option (a), numbers of lines inside the figure is equal to the sides of the figure drawn.
25. *(d)* Except option (d), drawn circles on the lines are facing in opposite direction.

What Comes Next?

1. *(c)* In the given pattern a letter is added according to the English alphabetical series and each bucket contains letter according to its position.

   (V) bucket has → 5P

   i.e. PPPPP
2. *(d)* Sequence shows alternate names of the weeks.
3. *(b)* Letters in the umbrella are arranged in increasing alphabetical order, but two letter is skipped in between two umbrella.
4. *(c)* In the given pattern third letter is removed from the Ist to get IInd cap. Follow the same pattern for the IIIrd to IVth cap.
5. *(b)* In the given pattern letters are arranged in increasing alphabetical order to form a group of 4 letters.
6. *(d)* The letters are given in backward order.
7. *(b)* Sequence shows alternate names of the months.
8. *(d)* Last letter is repeated two times in figure A i.e. K.
9. *(b)* In all the sun 3 digit numbers are in ascending order.

$$101 \xrightarrow{+101} 202 \xrightarrow{+101} 303 \xrightarrow{+101} \boxed{404}$$

10. *(c)* The pattern is follows as,

As, $12 - 3 = 9$

$9 - 3 = 6$

$6 - 3 = 3$

Here, all the numbers are arranged in decreasing order by 3.

11. *(b)* The pattern is follows as

As, '7' is written as '700'

Similarly, '5' is written as '500'.

12. (c) The pattern is follows as

As, 'Ten' is written as '10'.

Similarly, 'Nine' is written as '9'.

13. (d) Each time number is increased by 3 or follow the table of 3.

14. *(b)* Numbers in A are multiple of 3 and numbers in C are multiple of 1.
Similarly, numbers in B are multiple of 2.

15. *(c)* In every new figure, one new line appears.

16. *(d)* After third figure, pattern is repeated. So, second figure will be next figure.

17. *(c)* Number of cartoons decreased by 2 in every next figure.

18. *(b)* First and second figures are opposite to each other, third and fourth figure opposite to each other. Similarly, sixth figure will be opposite of fifth figure.

19. *(c)* Each time the circle and the square is increased by one.

20. *(c)* Each time the small square moves one block forward.

21. *(b)* After third figure, series is repeated.

22. *(c)* Each time one circle is added.

23. *(b)* Each object changes its position from vertical to horizontal direction.

24. *(c)* A new line is added in each step.

25. *(b)* After second figure, outer shape is repeated and one triangle is added in every step.

Complete the Figures

1. *(c)* Option figure (c) complete the given picture. It will look as shown below.

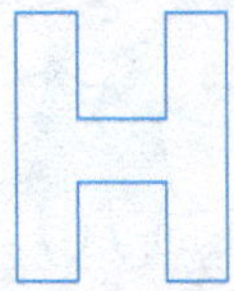

2. *(c)* Option figure (c) complete the given picture. It will look as shown below.

3. *(c)* Option complete (c) the given picture. It will look as shown below.

4. *(a)* Option figure (a) complete the given picture. It will look as shown below.

5. *(d)* Option figure (d) complete the given picture. It will look as shown below.

6. *(a)* Option figure (a) complete the given picture. It will look as shown below.

7. *(d)* Option figure (d) complete the given picture. It will look as shown below.

8. *(c)* Option figure (c) complete the given picture. It will look as shown below.

9. *(b)* Option figure (b) complete the given picture. It will look as shown below.

10. *(b)* Option figure (b) complete the given picture. It will look as shown below.

11. *(d)* Option figure (d) complete the pattern. It will look as shown below.

12. *(c)* Option figure (c) complete the pattern. It will look as shown below.

13. *(a)* Option figure (a) complete the pattern. It will look as shown below.

14. *(d)* Option figure (d) complete the pattern. It will look as shown below.

15. *(b)* Option figure (b) complete the given picture. It will look as shown below.

16. *(c)* Option figure (c) complete the given figure. It will look as shown below.

17. *(b)* Option figure (b) complete the given figure. It will look as shown below.

18. *(a)* Option figure (a) complete the given figure. It will look as shown below.

19. *(d)* Option figure (d) complete the given figure. It will look as shown below.

20. *(b)* Option figure (b) complete the given figure. It will look as shown below.

21. *(a)* Option figure (a) complete the given figure. It will look as shown below.

22. *(d)* Option figure (d) complete the given figure. It will look as shown below.

23. *(d)* Option figure (d) complete the given figure. It will look as shown below.

Find Similar Shapes

1. *(d)* Object (d) is same as the given figure.

2. *(c)* Object (c) is same as the given figure.

3. *(c)* Object (c) is same as the given figure.

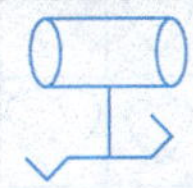

4. *(b)* Object (b) is same as the given figure.

5. *(c)* Object (c) is same as the given figure.

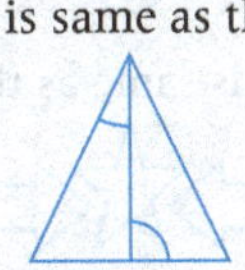

6. *(b)* Object (b) is same as the given figure.

7. *(d)* Object (d) is same as the given figure.

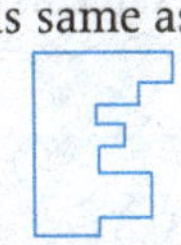

8. *(b)* Object (b) is same as the given figure.

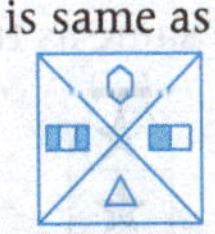

9. *(c)* Object (c) is same as the given figure.

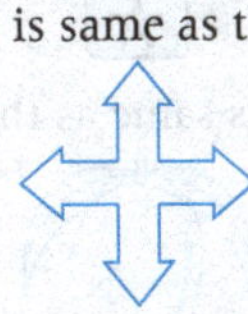

10. *(c)* Object (c) is same as the given figure.

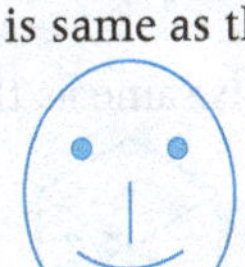

11. *(a)* Object (a) is same as the given figure.

12. *(b)* Object (b) is same as the given figure.

13. *(c)* Object (c) is same as the given figure.

14. *(d)* Object (d) is same as the given figure.

15. *(b)* Object (b) is same as the given figure.

16. *(a)* Object (a) is same as the given figure.

17. *(b)* Object (b) is same as the given figure.

18. *(c)* Object (c) is same as the given figure.

19. *(c)* Object (c) is same as the given figure.

20. *(b)* Object (b) is same as the given figure.

Grouping of Figures

1. *(c)* Triangle 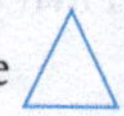 is present in the given group.

2. *(d)* Option (d)  is present in given group of toy.

3. *(c)* Smiley of option (c)  belongs to the given group.

4. *(b)* Toffee  is present in the given group.

5. *(c)* The given figure 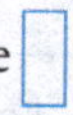 belongs to the group (c).

6. *(c)* There are 3 groups of 3 flowers.

7. *(b)* There are 5 equal groups of 5 triangles.

8. *(b)* There are 4 group of 6 straws.

9. *(b)*

10. *(d)*

11. *(c)* There are 3 groups of four eggs.

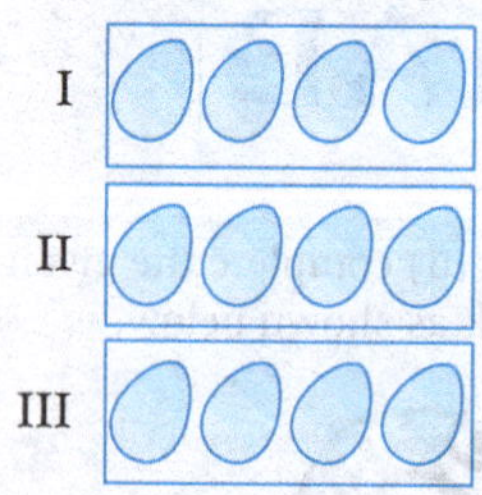

12. *(c)* There is 3 groups of 5 balloons.

13. *(a)* There are 4 house in each group.

14. *(a)* The object in option (a) is exactly the same as the figure shown in Group 2.

15. *(a)* The object in option (a) is exactly same as the figure shown in group I (a) i.e.

16. *(d)* The shapes in figures A and B are different from each other by shape and size.

17. *(c)* Group X Group Y Group Z

18. *(c)* There are 6 apples in the given figure.

Hence, number of Groups are of 6 apples = 3 Groups

19. *(d)* There are 7 carrots are present in the diagram.

20. *(a)* Total number of brinjals =2

Total number of peas = 4

Total number of brinjal less than pea are

$= 4 - 2 = 2$

Hence, 2 brinjals are less than peas in the diagram.

21. *(a)* Total number of tomatoes = 4

Total number of cauliflowers = 3

Total number of brinjal more than cauliflower $= 4 - 3 = 1$

Hence, only 1 tomato is more than cauliflower.

Hidden Figures

1. *(a)* Shape of option (a) is hidden in part 3.

2. *(b)* The shape given in the question is hidden in part 7.

3. *(d)* Two pictures are hidden in part 7.

4. *(b)* There are 10 eyes in part 4.

5. *(b)* The shape given in the question is hidden in part 6.

6. *(b)* Shape of option (b) is hidden in part 3.

7. *(c)* There are 2 stands in part 7.

8. *(d)* The given shape is hidden in option (d).

9. *(d)* The given shape is hidden in option (d).

10. *(c)* The given shape is hidden in option (c).

11. *(b)* The given shape is hidden in option (b).

12. *(a)* The given shape is hidden in option (a).

13. *(b)* The shape given in the question is hidden in part 6.

14. *(d)* Shape of option (d) is hidden in part 4.

Position Test

1. *(d)* W is the fourth letter from the right end.

2. *(d)* 5th number from the right end is 3 and 2nd number from the right end is 2, then $3 - 2 = 1$. So, 1 is the 3rd number from the left end.

3. *(b)* 1st number from the left end is 3 and 4th number from the left end is 4, then $3 + 4 = 7$. So, 7 is 2nd from the right end.

4. *(a)* If there is no 'L' in the given word, then Y is the 3rd letter from the left end.

5. *(c)* Monkey A is fifth from the left end.

6. *(c)* Image in option (c) is 3rd from the right end.

7. *(a)* Cap C is 7th from the left end.

8. *(a)* Fruit basket L is 8th from the right end.

9. *(b)* The position of the circle is 3rd from the left end.

10. *(b)* The position of arrow is 4th from the left end.

11. *(c)* When there is no mango in the given figure, then the apple is the 1st item from the right end.

12. *(a)* If there is no car in the given picture, then the cake is now the 3rd item from the left end.

13. *(d)* If we destroy house no. 4 then the position of house no. 7 from the left end is 6th.

14. *(d)* The position of car in circle is 5th from the left end.

15. *(d)* 3rd from the right end person is thinking something.

16. *(b)* The position of train having 2 bogey is 1st from the left end.

17. *(b)* Balloon M is between balloon P and balloon S.

18. *(d)* First balloon from the left end and first balloon from the right end are balloon A and balloon F.

19. (b) Pooja is in between Sunny and Jay.

20. (a) Mini is climbing on the top.

21. (b) Sunny is climbing just after Mini.

22. *(d)* Mahima is between Pooja and Rohan.

23. *(c)* Gitika is third in the given row.

24. *(d)* There are 5 children in the given row.

25. *(d)* Pooja is just after Gitika.

Practice Set-01

1. *(b)* Option figure (b) comes next in the series i.e.

2. *(a)* The given figure  belongs to group R.

3. *(b)* The position of car having '1 boy' is 4th from the right end.

4. *(d)* In option (d), the shape  is hidden.

5. *(d)* Option (d) figure exactly same as the given figure.

6. *(c)* 'E' is sixth from the right end.

7. *(d)* In part '5' the shape is hidden.

8. *(d)* Shape in option (d) is hidden in part 7.

9. *(b)* Two pictures are hidden in the part 3.

10. *(b)* Option (b) figure is different from others as, 'Circle' is not made by line while all other figures are made by line.

11. *(b)* Option figure (b) comes next.

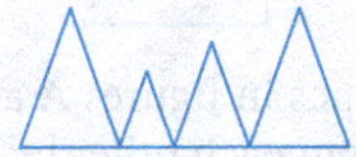

12. *(d)* Option figure (d) is different from other as it has two arrow while others have only one arrow.

13. *(a)* Circle is 4th from the left end according to the given condition.

14. *(b)* As, D^{E}_{C} = CDE

Similarly, N^{O}_{M} = MNO

15. *(d)* Option (d) completes the given figure.

16. *(d)* 6 groups of 3 cones can be formed from the figures.

17. *(c)* Option figure (c) completes the second pair.

18. *(d)* Pencil in option (d) is different from others.

19. *(d)* Letter 'L' is third from the left end.

20. *(a)* Option figure (a) completes the pattern of the second pair.

21. *(c)* As, Six is written as '6'.

Similarly, Seven is written as '7'.

22. *(b)* Each time the cost of butterfly is increased by 5.

$$30 \xrightarrow{+5} 35 \xrightarrow{+5} 40 \xrightarrow{+5} \boxed{45}$$

So, the option (b) is correct.

23. *(b)* Option (b) completes the given figure.

24. *(b)* Option (b) object is same as the given figure.

25. *(d)* There are 4 equal groups of 6 glass of juice.

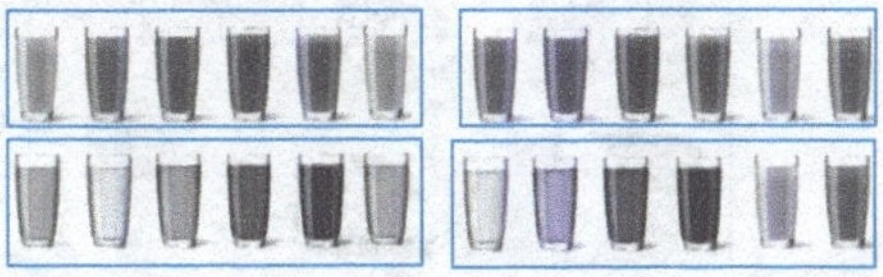

26. *(c)* The given shape  is hidden in option (c).

27. *(d)*  is 4th letter from the left end.

28. *(b)* The pattern is as follows
1 star, 1 triangle, 1 square. Here 1 triangle is missing.

29. *(c)* Option (c) completes the given number.

30. *(c)* Option (c) object is same as the given figure.

31. *(c)* The object in option (c) is belongs to the group II i.e.

32. *(d)* The pattern is follows as
P is moved two step forward to get-R and so on…
So, we get, $X \xrightarrow{+2} \boxed{Z}$

33. *(d)* Option (d) completes the given word. The word is Kite.

34. *(c)* Option (c) image is hidden in the given figure.

35. *(d)* The position of Evan is 4th.

Practice Set-02

1. *(c)* As, Doctors have stethoscope, similarly sewing woman have sewing machine.

2. *(b)* The given series is in increasing order of the months i.e. August comes at the place of question mark.

3. *(d)* Option figure (d) is same as the given figure.

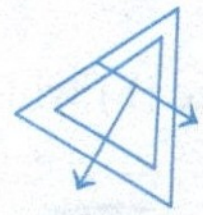

4. *(d)* Except option (d), the subtraction of the given number is always 2.
But in option (d), (15 − 5 = 10).

5. *(b)* Second figure is made by the lines given in first figure.

6. *(c)* Candle K is between X and L.

7. *(b)* The position of shortest candle is 5th from the left end.

8. *(c)* The shortest and longest candles are 'K' and 'T'.

9. *(b)* ① [2] is comes next, as circle and square, comes alternatively with the addition of 2.

$04 \xrightarrow{+2} 06 \xrightarrow{+2} 08 \xrightarrow{+2} 10 \xrightarrow{+2} \boxed{12}$

10. *(a)* The shape  belongs to group 'B' and 'D'.

11. *(d)* Figure (d) is same as the given figure.

12. *(b)* Option (b) is other half part of the given figure.

13. *(d)* As 'USN' is ''. Similarly, 'THA' is ''.

14. *(d)* The position of number in the circle is 5th from the left end.

15. *(c)* The position of 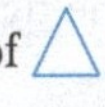 from the right end is 6th.

16. *(c)* The given series is increasing in alphabetical order. So, 'GHI' comes on question mark.

17. *(a)* In option (a), given shape is hidden.

18. *(c)* '08' is different from others.

19. *(a)* 'GHIJ' will replace the question mark as here increasing order of alphabetical series is given.

20. *(b)* Option figure (b) will complete the given figure pattern.

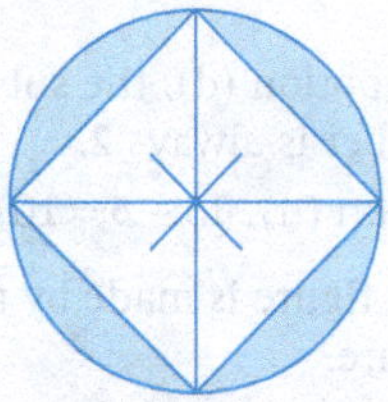

21. *(d)* As, 8 is written as 800.
Similarly, 9 is written as 900.

22. *(d)* Except option (d), all are used to eat food. while option (d) used for straining purpose.

23. *(a)* From the alternatives we see that, the figure in option (a) will complete the given pattern. It will look as shown below.

24. *(d)* Option figure (d) is exactly same as question figure.

25. *(d)* The position of encircled chair is 4th.

26. *(b)* There are 2 group of 3 females.

27. *(c)* Option (c) object is same as the given figure.

28. *(c)* The objects in figures (A) and (B) are different from each other by quantity in 'figure A' there are '11 kites' and in 'figure B' there are only '7 kites'.

29. *(c)* Shape in option (c) is hidden in part 7.

30. *(c)* In part '6' of the figure shape is hidden.

31. *(d)*

Hence, '5' pictures are hidden in the part '8'.

32. *(b)* All except 'SUNDAY' are months of year. Hence, option (b) is odd one.

33. *(d)* Option (d) completes the given number.

34. *(c)* Deepa is standing in the middle of the queue.

35. *(c)* There are 5 fish given in the figure.